GW00457109

Stop Overthinking

A Guide to Eliminate Excessive Thinking. Practical Techniques and Small Habits to Alleviate Anxiety, Remove Thoughts and Achieve Peace

By

PHILIP GIBSON

Philip Gibson

Philip Gibson has dedicated his life to writing self-help books and helping people overcome internal conflicts, acquire emotional intelligence to manage their emotions, and achieve their goals.

Born and raised in a modest family, Philip showed great interest in psychology and emotional well-being from a young age. After completing his studies, he began working as a personal advisor and mental coach.

Later on, he decided to transmit his knowledge and experience to people through writing. He published his first self-help book at the age of 39, which was a great success among the public.

Since then, he has continued to write numerous personal growth books on topics such as stress management, self-confidence, happiness, motivation, and overthinking. Thanks to his publications, he has reached thousands of people worldwide who have benefited from his advice and techniques.

If you want to share your opinion and enter to win a Kindle on "how to increase productivity", scan this QR Code using your phone's camera or go directly to this link:

www.philipgibsonbooks.com

DEDICATION

To everyone out there feeling hurt, lost or alone,
and trying their best to make things better

Table of Contents

Introduction

What does your mind transmit to you most consistently? If you have been interested in reading this writing, it is probably just negativity, worrying thoughts, and fear.

Is this the case?

Is your internal dialogue usually negative and encouraging your worries?

Do you reflect too much on the problems that come your way? Are you constantly thinking about the past or some problem, or foreseeing the future, and you can't stop, even if you try? Before making a decision, do you think over and over again, which ends up making you procrastinate making that decision? Do you find it hard to sleep at night because you spend too much time staring at the ceiling, thinking negative thoughts of various kinds? Could it be said that your mind controls you instead of you controlling your mind? Can't you turn your mind off, even if you try? Is overthinking affecting your daily life? Is it preventing you from enjoying your present, or is it becoming an obstacle for you to do the activities you want to do? That's what overthinking is all about.

Do you need it to stop? Surely, it's something you crave.

I dare say that there is no adult in the world who has not experienced someday in their life what it is like to ruminate with the mind, to overthink, to turn over one or several negative thoughts over and over and over again or, to a repetitive and limiting thought over and over again. That is why every adult knows the feeling of being unable to control automatic thoughts that come to mind with the apparent and only reason to worry or torment.

What human being likes problems? None, of course. So, the most humane thing to do in their presence is to think of a solution. The key is to be able to stop thinking about the problem, even if no such solution is found despite having thought of one. Still, if it is impossible to get the problem out of your mind and it relives it every hour to the point of taking away sleep or affecting the day-to-day, then it becomes a distressing situation. Instead of obtaining the desired calm by finding the solution to the conflict, one experiences more confusion and anguish... A great discomfort and anxiety.

When the thought becomes too repetitive and distressing, it is no longer positive for the solution of the problem. We can't think of a good solution to a conflict when we are worried or fearful; overthinking does not have a good reason to be.

The common thing to do when making an important decision is to think about the pros and cons of the options you have. Still, if the thought becomes recurrent to the point of preventing you from making the decision instead of helping you to make it, then it is something that generates discomfort and is detrimental.

Everyone knows a person with low self-esteem, or some have been that person with low self-esteem who assumes the worst.

Let's suppose it's your sister's birthday (the person you know with low self-esteem), it's 6:00 in the evening, and she hasn't received a congratulatory message, a call or any detail from her boyfriend, and she starts to think the worst, what if something happened to him? What if I made him angry and I didn't notice? What if he doesn't love me? What if he left me for someone else? And you find that your sister can't stop wondering all these things even though you try to console her by telling her that he is probably still in classes where he is forbidden to use a cell phone, resulting at the end that this is the truth.

Most probably, you are or have been that person who does not stop thinking about terrible scenarios in a situation, and, most likely, some of the times you were immersed in worry, it turned out to be unnecessary because nothing terrible was happening; it was all in your mind.

These are clear examples of what is involved in overthinking. These represent a pattern from the day-to-day life of a person who never stops thinking, imagining in the negative, turning over a disturbing idea, and being unable to act because of overthinking.

Society has been instilled with the idea that thinking too much is a good sign, a positive characteristic, and a sign of being rational. But this is not always the truth because there are also irrational thoughts based only on beliefs and fears, which have no real or entirely rational basis.

The excessive thinking that this paper presents is toxic. Not being able to stop thinking about everything until the thoughts become distressing means that you cannot stop thinking every day about life situations such as those in the examples above. A day by day full of negative and distressing thoughts, unable to stop the mind from thinking negatively, living in anguish or fear because of ideas that do not stop arising. It has to do with thoughts that evoke negative emotions, that contribute nothing, that add up to nothing.

Any person must have experienced this pattern of behavior either in the face of a conflict or on the eve of having to face a situation that scares him, that takes him away from his comfort zone, a stressful situation. There is a tendency in human beings to think a lot; it has been instilled in them that they must think twice about things.

The most natural attitude, when faced with a situation that makes us nervous, is to think of the worst that can happen because that is a consequence of fear, although those who are more secure or confident do not usually have to face that problem as much. The natural attitude before taking an important decision is to think about it, but if in any situation one cannot stop wondering, or it is impossible not to mentally conceive the worst and constantly thinking and thinking about it over and over again, this becomes overthinking, a recurrent and negative way of thinking that invades the mind and increases the fear or limits. IT IS NOT CONVENIENT, AND IT IS HARMFUL. It really complicates your life and prevents you from enjoying it.

What if I forget what I have to say in my speech? What if my belt comes off in the middle of my speech, and my pants come down? What if everyone makes fun of me? What if it goes wrong? What if I am left alone? What if...? What if...?

It is difficult to live in the present and enjoy life because of overthinking about a future that will probably never materialize, in a situation that, if it happens as we think it will probably not be as terrible as we imagine (almost nothing is as terrible as we imagine, the truth is that imagination magnifies the consequences of problems or unwanted situations).

We can talk about excessive thinking as a problem to be faced when there is difficulty stopping, when we think so many things that it becomes a labyrinth with no way out, an obstacle to action, a wall to carry out activities, anxiety, or panic attacks.

If this attitude decreases, if the thoughts are reduced before the solution of the conflict that was faced or, after having overcome the stressful situation, we can not speak of a problem, the problem arises when it becomes a habit to think too much and negatively, which can affect even the health and quality of life.

Is it habitual for you to ruminate on your thoughts to the point of becoming overly distressed?

If it has become a habit for you to overthink all the time, even if you try not to, if overthinking takes away even your sleep and motivation, it is understandable that you are looking for a solution because, undoubtedly, thinking too much and negatively brings discomfort, it is basically self-torture. And that's because the ideas we generate in our brain influence how we feel. If you think positively you will feel positive and good, but if you live in constant anguish in your mind, you will feel anxious, fearful, and grumpy.

It is not possible to feel good with a mind full of negative thoughts that trigger perennial anguish; this leads to stress and can also make the body sick because the mind and the body stay connected. It is no secret that stress is often the prelude to chronic diseases of all kinds. The connection between the mind and the body is supported by science, so too much negativity in your mind can make you sick.

For sure, you do not want to get sick because of your mind, and this is a fact because if you have been interested in this text, you are looking for a solution. You want to find peace of mind, to be able to control your thoughts, to stop overthinking if you choose to. You want to transform your life and live it without fear and with wellness, and the solution in this book will help you transform your mind and overcome the bad habit of overthinking and negativity. You have probably tried to solve it on your own, but without success; maybe you have tried to suppress those unwanted ideas without any effective result. It's not just about suppressing those thoughts; that doesn't work. Overcoming excessive thinking involves a transformative process, a series of techniques, changes, relearning, and acquiring new habits.

I want to let you know first of all that you are not alone in this problem. Overthinking is like stress, which has been baptized as the evil of the modern age since too many people experience it. Like with stress, many people acquire the pattern of overthinking as a habit. It is more common than you might think because we all experience fear and distress and, due to our beliefs or experiences, can't always deal with it effectively.

If one does not fight to take control of the mind, the mind ends up being in control, and when it is the mind that is in control, it tends to give free rein to negative thoughts as a defense mechanism, activate anxiety as a way of dealing with what it considers to be an imminent danger, even though there is no such danger. Or to make us anxious. That's what the mind does when we leave it on automatic.

We have to take control; that's what it's all about. You overthink because you have given too much control to your mind; you have to take it back, and that is not only about knowing that you need to be in control. As I have told you before, changes are needed, and modifications of this kind require a process. Don't be frustrated if you have tried to free yourself from overthinking without success; you have not succeeded simply because you lacked the reasoning you will find in this book.

Busy modern life can trigger stress and can lead to overthinking if you don't learn to control your mind and thoughts. There are also other causes of overthinking, such as low self-esteem, pessimism, or a tendency to perfectionism. Regardless of how the habit of thinking too much about yourself was born, this text aims to help you overcome it and to understand in depth the problem that causes you discomfort.

The fact is that you need to overcome recurrent negative overthinking if you want to recover your well-being, and you DESERVE TO RECOVER IT, right? You deserve peace of mind, of course, you do.

If overthinking has become a habit for you and you live in stress, worry no more. This is a book that brings healing. It is not a magical solution that these letters allude to, I must warn you. This book presents a solution that will require your commitment because there is no person that can defeat and control your mind, only you. But, if you commit yourself fully, you will defeat those invasive ideas once and for all, and by your own means, you will attract positivity and peace in your life, the one you need so much, the one that will help you to live your days with more plenitude. This writing will serve as a guide for you to achieve it.

You can overcome excessive negative thinking because it is a habit and a vice, and, just as there is no invincible habit, just as anyone can leave behind cigarettes or alcohol, you can control your mind and overcome the habit of ruminating with your thoughts if you set your mind to it and follow the tips and techniques you will learn below.

Read on to enter the wonderful path of knowledge that will lead you to your peace of mind. It will be my honor to accompany you in this process.

I know how it feels. I understand how you feel because I experienced overthinking firsthand; my negativity controlled me, and I could not find peace. But, thanks to the techniques and tips that I will be revealing, I was able to transform my beliefs, free myself from my fears and find peace of mind. That brought me so much peace and well-being that I want everyone who suffers from this same condition to be able to overcome it.

Without further ado, let's start this journey of transformation together:

Commitment

Before we begin, please make a sincere commitment to yourself. Remember that the good results that this transformational process will bring will depend largely on your commitment to follow the advice you will find in this writing and with your perseverance. I have already said it in previous lines, and I emphasize it as you are the only owner of your mind, the only one who can control it; it will depend on you to dominate it to overcome excessive thinking. Of course, some professionals can help you achieve this, but they can only guide you; they cannot control your mind for you.

"I commit myself to learn how to combat overthinking, not to stay with the knowledge acquired, to apply in my life the techniques described in this writing, and to seek that peace that I deserve and need.

I will follow this path with faith until the transformation of my own life and to be able to control my mind."

What Is Overthinking?

To overcome overthinking, we must first understand what it is.

Excessive thinking is also known as overthinking precisely because it implies just that, overthinking in excess or uncontrollably. Not being able to stop thinking, turning situations over and over again until you even lose sleep.

Imagine that in your mind, there is a switch that you can turn on and off at will whenever you imagine situations. Based on that, imagine that you start having negative ideas that cause you distress, then you flip the off switch when you want to stop, and nothing happens; it doesn't turn off, and your mind fills uncontrollably with pessimistic thoughts that fill you with anxiety, guilt, stress. This is excessive thinking, and not being able to stop doing it is as if it were a vice that you could not just get rid of.

Thinking is a human activity that is normally related to study and intelligence. No one conceives thinking as something negative until negative overthinking arrives, until one cannot stop thinking, until an inner voice appears throughout the day, at the most unexpected moments, to encourage fears or negative assumptions, to remind us that there is a problem we must solve to which we have not found a solution, to tell us of a frightening future, to punish us for actions we did in the past.

Everything would be different if positive overthinking existed and if our mind could not stop thinking optimistically, but overthinking as a problem to face does not work that way; it is precisely a problem because it is negative; it only submerges us in negativity, pessimism, fear, in nervousness, in discomfort.

Excessive thinking implies overthinking the worst, creating catastrophic scenarios, getting involved in a labyrinth of discouraging reflections, and finding it difficult to get out of such a labyrinth and free oneself. It usually involves thinking about an idea or a group of ideas or considerations repeatedly and not being able to stop doing this. It is to think chronically.

Are You A Chronic Thinker?

To take into account: Before starting the topic, I consider it necessary to clarify that the word "chronic refers to something deep-rooted, something that lasts over time". It should not be associated with a disease, at least as far as this book and its topic are concerned.

If you still have doubts about overthinking or if this type of behavior can be considered a problem, you should face and read the following characteristics. If you feel identified with one or some of them, you are undoubtedly a chronic overthinker; thinking too much is doing its thing with you, it is affecting your daily life, robbing you of your peace of mind, and harming you. It has become an ingrained habit in you:

- You find it hard to sleep, or you wake up at night because of repetitive thoughts that worry or distress you, and this is something you have become accustomed to.

- Before making a decision, you think about it a thousand times, which often prevents you from taking action.

- When you have a task, you can't stop thinking about how to do it because you need it to be perfect, which often leads you to procrastinate. (You find it difficult to finish your tasks because you can't stop thinking about how to do them or what would happen if you do them wrong).

- You are always mentally creating catastrophic scenarios for yourself, and you think about them all day.

- You always think the worst.

- You tend to minimize and underestimate yourself: "I won't be able to," "I'm not capable," and similar thoughts often haunt your mind.

- You question what other people do as if you can read their minds and, almost always, in the negative, which makes you very affected by what others do because you take it personally. An example of this tendency would be to think like this:

Two of your friends go out to have fun without you, then you think they are probably not your real friends, that they don't want to be with you anymore, that they don't really like you, that they did it specifically to see you suffer. A whole lot of self-torture.

- You constantly question your actions and think about what would have happened if you had acted differently (you tend to judge yourself).

- Your mind usually dwells on past actions that make you feel guilty about something you did or happened some time ago.

- You are too tormented by what people will say to the point that you constantly think about it.

Identifying the problem is the first step to the solution. If you are a chronic thinker, it is crucial that you detect it, that you can see your problem, and that you accept it because it is from this acceptance that the commitment you need to make to overcome the bad habit of overthinking in the negative can be born.

At this point, you can answer yourself honestly: Are you or are you not a chronic thinker? Is overthinking a problem that you should solve?

Do you have the answer?

If you really are a chronic overthinker and you want to find a solution continue reading.

What Caused the Excessive Thoughts That Haunt You Every Day?

Before addressing this point, I consider it necessary to highlight a characteristic of excessive negative and irrational thoughts: THEY ARE AUTOMATIC. You cannot stop your mind from creating them, which implies that it is NOT YOUR FAULT.

Possibly some readers, when coming across the title: "Causes of Excessive Thoughts," are expecting to find that they are responsible, but that is not the case. What you can do with automatic negative and worrying thoughts is manage them. What you lack is learning to take control. Sure, some ways of thinking or habits may encourage your mind to create those kinds of ideas, but nothing is wrong with you because that happens; don't think that way because it will only hurt you. Instead, think about the positive things that you are doing right now, trying to improve and transform your life. It is a great sign of the desire for self-improvement and self-esteem that must be emphasized. Having clarified the above, let's continue with the causes.

Everyone is different, but specific triggers tend to unleash overthinking. I'll delve into them below, as it's crucial for you to discover the reason for your predicament so you can more efficiently address it in the search for a solution.

Understanding why what happens to us is never a waste of time; it can always be used in the search for solutions and improvement.

Poor Management of Emotions

Emotional intelligence is the ability of human beings to correctly manage their negative emotions: to control their anger, anguish, fear, and thus prevent these emotions from taking over.

Without emotional intelligence, or the ability to manage emotions, fears and anxieties become bigger than they really are, and the mind enlarges them.

Commonly behind the problem of excessive thinking, there is a fear that has not been mastered. It is fear that makes people think up catastrophic scenarios that very rarely happen in reality or that, if they do happen, are not as terrible as they were thought, but, in the mind, they hurt, cause anxiety, rigidity, and limiting.

Fear is a very important defense mechanism of the mind when activated for the right reasons. In the face of imminent danger, it can save your life, and it can help you act quickly to escape or defend yourself from the damage that real danger can cause you, but when danger exists only in the mind, fear is negative, paralyzing and limiting for no reason.

The natural reaction to having to face something that terrifies us is to think. For those who have not acquired emotional intelligence, it will mean thinking the worst: "If I leave the house alone for one night, it will catch fire; if I talk to that person I want to meet, they will make fun of me; if I try I will fail; if I do it wrong I will be a loser; I will lose my job, etc."

A lack of emotion management leads to a maze of thoughts like the above.

Do you perceive the world as a frightening place where many are out to harm you and where anything terrible can happen at any moment? Is your mind hardly in the present and, instead, constantly traveling to a negative future? If this is the case, most probably, the lack of management of your emotions is the trigger of your overthinking problem.

To free yourself from the chain of excessive thoughts, you will need to develop emotional intelligence, above all, to keep negativity out of your mind and your life.

Stress

Suppose you live your life in a hectic way, leaving aside recreation and relaxation activities and demanding more and more of yourself. In that case, it is very likely that the trigger of your excessive thoughts is stress produced by an enormous self-demand.

Stress usually activates natural responses in the body, one of which is anxiety.

Anxiety due to excessive pressure or a very stressful life will keep your mind full of thoughts that will stress you even more: "I have to solve such and such a problem," "I need to finish this soon; if I don't finish it soon I will have problems," "I must do this, I must do that," "Would it have been better if I did such and such a way and not this way," "What if I don't do it right"?

When your mind is filled with thoughts like those in the above examples, it implies that you are leading a hectic lifestyle or that you are over-exerting yourself.

If the trigger for your excessive thoughts is none other than your busy lifestyle, you must, above all, learn to moderate it and give priority to activities that calm or relax you to overcome your problem and free yourself from the labyrinth of thoughts that torment you once and for all.

Responsibilities are important, but so is mental health, which is weakened when you don't make time for recreational activities and relaxation. You will have to make time for them and make time for yourself, for your own good.

Need to Be in Control

- Tendency to Perfectionism or, Chronic Perfectionism: People with perfectionist personality traits tend to develop the habit of ruminating with the mind, of overthinking. This, in the pursuit of reaching their own standards of perfection that are practically impossible.

Are you a perfectionist, and do you find it hard to let go of control because you think that if you don't do all the things that need to be done, they won't be done correctly?

You should know that perfection is not inherent to being human; on the contrary. Being human implies making mistakes sometimes, and that's okay because mistakes are where learning and personal development come from. If there is no mistake, there is no learning; you must keep that in mind.

If you are obsessed with being in control, with achieving perfection, then your mind will work for it by overthinking, always working to make you believe that the worst can happen if you delegate or if you don't do something as perfect as it can be, always pushing you to judge yourself harshly, making you feel guilty if you think you are not giving enough of yourself, submerging you in stress... All this unnecessarily, all this based on the fear you have hidden inside you, the fear of failing, of being wrong.

It is not a matter of doing things for the sake of doing them, of not seeking excellence; excellence can be achieved, but not perfection. The path to excellence is reached by learning, making mistakes, rectifying, and moving forward. Not so, perfection, which would imply practically not making mistakes, not allowing oneself to make them.

Perfectionist people live in stress because their minds and dominant thoughts lead them to impose on themselves the heavy burden of having everything under control, which would be similar to carrying the duty of the celestial vault on their shoulders.

Of course, this tendency was born somewhere. Normally perfectionist people are so because in their childhood, perfection was demanded of them; it is difficult for them not to set standards to follow because ingrained in them is the belief that they must do everything perfectly, and this became a habit, but, there is neither a limiting belief nor a bad habit that cannot be overcome. And, if your overthinking problem is due to an inhuman tendency towards perfectionism, you will have to overcome that bad habit.

If you find it hard to let go, to delegate; if you think that if you don't go to work one day, everything will go wrong, that if you leave a task in someone else's hands, it will be ruined, that if you make a mistake something terrible may happen. The need for control and your tendency to seek perfection is hurting you and most likely causing you excessive thoughts that you want to get away from your life.

Nobody is perfect, not even the person you admire the most and who seems the most perfect to you. If you believe you can achieve perfection, you will be in an eternal search for something that no person can achieve. The perfection you want to achieve is only that way because you have convinced yourself of it; you have created your own standard of perfection based on your own beliefs. To free yourself from the excessive thinking that has arisen from this cause, you will need, above all, to learn to let go, to become a little more flexible, to free yourself from the need to control, from the limiting and cruel belief that makes you think that you always need to be in control, that you need to make everything perfect.

Pessimism

It is difficult for an excessively negative person not to end up succumbing to the torment of excessive thoughts because people with this tendency are always thinking the worst, seeing the negative side of every thing or person, and expecting the worst of the situations they have to face; in their mind there is negativity. In previous lines, I have already made reference to the fact that excessive thoughts, as a problem, are negative. There is no self-torture or torment, and there is no lack of sleep or discomfort from overthinking positively, but there is from thinking excessively negative.

"What is going to happen if inflation goes on like this?" "How am I going to subsist if the price of the dollar skyrockets?" "How terrible, a cyclone is coming, and the rains may destroy my house." There is no peace of mind in the mind of a person prone to pessimism; pessimism invades everything.

If you are pessimistic and your excessive thoughts are related to it, you must learn to change your perspective and overcome or push away a little negativity from your life and mentality in order to overcome it.

Low Self-Esteem

It is not uncommon for excessive thoughts to hide low self-esteem.

People with low self-esteem often focus on what people will say, worry about being judged, or are always thinking the worst about themselves or the worst-case scenario.

Their lack of confidence creates uncertainty, and that uncertainty leads them to overthink.

"He didn't greet me on the street; did I do something to make him angry?" "What will people think of me if they find out X thing?" "Will I be good enough at X thing?" "I'm not capable; I'll do

poorly."

If you are trapped in excessive thoughts due to low self-appreciation, you will have to work primarily on your self-esteem to overcome this problem.

Negative attitudes of reference figures: Many causes of overthinking, such as the tendency to perfectionism or pessimism, arose from reference models.

Possibly your tendency to anguish or pessimism or your high standards of demand and perfection are due to the fact that, in your family, your parental figures, above all, also had a tendency to negativity, or they demanded a lot, or they demanded too much of you and pressured you to the point that you longed to be perfect as a child, and you grew up with that idea.

Therefore, I would like to invite you to realize that, if this is your case, those models did not benefit you, and it is not in your best interest to remain attached to them. They have a basis in your upbringing but do not have to accompany you for life. Read on to free yourself from any limiting belief, negative tendency, or anything that keeps you chained to overthinking. The beliefs that were instilled in you do not have to be your prison for life. Don't allow them to become your prison for life.

After reading this section, do you already know what caused your habit of overthinking or what usually triggers it? If not, I encourage you to find out and self-analyze. Dig into the nature of the negative thoughts that tend to invade your mind, and you will find out.

The nightmare for those who think too much: Nighttime

The arrival of the night usually represents fear for those who think too much because it makes it difficult to sleep. It is in the silence that comes with the hour of rest that chronic thinkers become more engrossed in their thoughts, when their mind is more active, when their inner voice seems to want to torture them more, when they start turning things over and over again, negative ideas over and over again.

Some find it hard to sleep; others wake up several times during the night and, after waking up, can't help but get caught in a tangle of unwanted thoughts. In any case, rest in this way is neither deep nor pleasant.

Do negative thoughts tend to repeatedly haunt your mind at night, preventing or hindering you from getting a peaceful rest? Do you identify with this situation?

Sleep should be a pleasurable activity for everyone because rest brings health and well-being. Restful sleep helps the body recover from the energy loss that occurred during the day. While we sleep, the body repairs damaged tissues, and the brain produces serotonin and melatonin, two hormones that counteract the hormones that trigger stress, adrenaline, and cortisol, therefore, it relaxes; sufficient sleep takes away the ravages of stress and anxiety.

Restorative sleep improves the immune system, gives mental clarity the next day, and promotes memory and quality of life. The opposite, insomnia, brings daytime sleepiness and impairs the performance of activities the next day, makes it difficult to concentrate, causes terrible moods, and encourages stress and anxiety. You can get sick if insomnia continues for a long time.

Overcoming the habit of overthinking will help you sleep better, with all the benefits it brings.

When you obtain the mental serenity that the process of overcoming excessive thinking brings with it, you will leave behind the fear of the hour of rest at night, it will cease to be the hour of torment, and the night will become the time of true restorative rest.

Why Overcome the Habit of Overthinking?

If you keep in mind the reasons why you should overcome your overthinking problem as soon as possible, you will feel more motivated as you walk the path of transformation and healing you need. Motivation will be very helpful; it will allow you to persevere because this will be a path of perseverance and determination that, if you do not give up, will lead you to achieve your desired goal. In that sense:

Overthinking Paralyzes; Overcoming This Bad Habit Will Liberate You From Such Limitation

Undoubtedly you abstain from much because of the doubts and anxiety that this bad habit causes you. Thinking too much in the negative implies that you have little tolerance for uncertainty or that you are too afraid. But, beyond all those doubts and fear, you have so much to experience; don't miss out on anything else. Life is short enough to deprive ourselves of dreams and experiences out of fear.

This is one of the most compelling reasons for you to set out to overcome this problem and to persevere until you do. Overcoming your problem of excessive thinking will imply that you live better, more fully, act when you want to act, and stop procrastinating or refusing to do things you want to do but do not do because of doubts and fear. It implies freeing yourself from chains that paralyze you, leaving behind limitations in favor of going for your dreams and those experiences you wanted to live but that your tendency to anxiety had not allowed you to do.

Peace of mind and deserved rest; you can conquer both by overcoming excessive thinking.

You have been suffering the anguish of overthinking for too long, haven't you?

The opposite of peace of mind is precisely anguish, and excessive thinking brings sorrow; it can trigger anxiety, insomnia, and discomfort. To all this, you can say goodbye if you find peace of mind. On the way to overcome excessive thinking, you will undoubtedly find it because one of the infallible ways to overcome it is precisely to learn to control thoughts and emotions to bring peace of mind and serenity to life.

You deserve peace of mind; with peace, you can better enjoy life's situations. Try to overcome excessive thinking so that you can conquer it.

What is the best thing that peace of mind will bring?

That you will be able to live in your present and, therefore, live to the fullest.

You Will Have Control of Your Mind, You Will Be Its True Master, and You Will No Longer Be Driven by Fear or any Negative Emotion

By overcoming excessive thinking, you will have conquered your mind. You will have learned how to command it and not the other way around; you will stop giving free rein to the tendency of the mind when we give it control: Thinking the worst, creating catastrophic scenarios, giving free rein to limiting beliefs, phobias, traumas, thinking blinded in all that, distorting reality, and in a negative way? By dominating your mind, on the other hand, you will be able to attract what you want: optimism, confidence, and serenity.

Your mind will no longer dominate you; it will no longer influence how you feel, preventing you from enjoying your present moment. By controlling your mind, you will be able to control your emotions as well. Hardly any negative emotion will come back to overwhelm you with unrealistic scenarios. You will feel more accessible than ever; you will have acquired emotional intelligence, which is the ability to handle any situation more rationally without being overwhelmed by unfavorable emotions.

Quality of Life and General Well-Being

Since overcoming overthinking will keep anguish and negativity out of your life, you can expect once you have overcome this self-torturing habit, you will have a higher quality of life and overall peace of mind.

The peace of mind that overcoming overthinking brings will fill you with health and motivation and lead you to enjoy life as you deserve.

Healthy Self-Esteem

Overcoming overthinking will also mean improvements in your self-esteem, stopping underestimating yourself, and gaining confidence.

Conquering a better self-esteem can lead you to achieve anything, and overcoming overthinking can lead you to it.

How to Free Your Mind and Develop Positive Attitudes?

Before all the information you have learned so far, you will be waiting for a how-to.

If you have come this far, you already understand more about the problem of overthinking and why you need to free your mind from it; all the beautiful things await you beyond that bad habit of overthinking and negative thinking. You know that you can free yourself, and you have to be waiting for the solution. As I have commented in previous lines, healing, in this case, comes from a process that will involve a transformation, changes in lifestyle, and the development of positive attitudes. Overcoming the negative to give way to the positive is a process that I will detail below. Get ready to begin to heal and live a life free of excessive harmful and intrusive thoughts.

Before I begin to delve into the various techniques and activities that can help you regain control of your mind and overcome the bad habit of overthinking, I must digress and ask you to believe in the healing power of this process. This requires your part of the commitment. When we believe in something, we give it power. If you follow this process without any faith at all, you will hardly give the following techniques the necessary compromise. I repeat, as I have pointed out in previous lines, this is not a miraculous process that will give you an immediate solution; it will be a step-by-step change, one day at a time. Before you know it, you will be healed, but you have to believe that you can and follow the advice in this paper with hope and determination.

There is a way out, but it will depend on you to get there. Think that if you do not believe that these techniques can help you, you will hardly be able to use them in your daily life, and if you do not persevere, you will not be able to overcome the bad habit of overthinking because every practice is deeply rooted in the human being and that is why you will find resistance. Your mind will resist changing its habitual way of proceeding, of deviating towards excessive thinking, you will be battling with it until you take control, until you win, until you achieve a healing transformation, until you have changed your perspective and developed more favorable habits. However, without faith, you will not persevere, or hardly persevere, and if you do not persevere, you will not be able to beat the ingrained habit in you.

However, it is most likely that you will find it hard to have faith in the process at the beginning, especially before you start or a few days after you start. If this is your case, follow the process anyway, and keep applying the advice you will find in this document. It is hard for humans to have faith without results, you will not get those results immediately, but with small changes, strategies, and new habits, you can control the negativity and anxiety that excessive thoughts can produce and feel better. These good results will help you to acquire faith, so if you really find it hard to believe what you have to do, follow the process in the same way, even without faith.

That said, without further ado, here is the step-by-step process towards your healing.

How to Eliminate Negativity

As long as you cannot get rid of negativity and pessimism, you will hardly be able to get rid of excessive thinking. Therefore, the following is a series of techniques or activities that will gradually help you to eradicate the negative.

Be the Doorman of Your Own Mind, Close the Access to the Negative Thoughts, and Transforming Them. Mental Conditioning Technique

It will not help you to try to suppress the repetitive negative thoughts in your mind just like that, so the solution is to transform them into favorable, positive thoughts, into concepts that will help you to fight the negativity of the negative thoughts that appear to want to torture you. Your task, in this case, will be to propose yourself to be the doorman of your own mind. Your job will be to be the one who decides which thoughts to give space to and which ones you should not feed. Those that do not suit you will have to fight them by means of other concepts that you consciously choose and that counteract them.

By constantly repeating positive ideas to counteract the negative ones, you can neutralize the effects of the negative thoughts. Remember that it has been commented in previous lines that these perceptions influence your emotions. By counteracting everything negative that appears in your mind, you will be able to keep away the negative emotions, fear, and anguish that any type of thought can make you experience, and, with this, it will be less probable that this thought will continue appearing in your mind. If it does, you must act in the same way, carry out this technique and be perseverant in it until you manage to condition your mind, convince it of the positive, and make it give up the negative idea that recurrently comes to your mind. This is a mental conditioning technique, a very useful one to change your perspective. Through it, you can overcome any bad habit, including overthinking.

It is very simple to carry out this technique; you just have to, every time an intrusive negative thought appears in your mind, stop for a moment to analyze it and look for a positive one that can counteract it. Then repeat the positive thought in your mind or out loud until you silence the negative thought that appeared without permission just to make you feel bad or fill you with negativity.

Suppose the negative intrusive thoughts that appear in your mind are the following: "I will do very poorly at the job interview tomorrow," "Surely more qualified people than me will go to the interview and they will get the job," "I will go to the interview to be embarrassed, what if I better not go and save myself the bad time?"

As the gatekeeper of your mind, when analyzing this thread of ideas, you will have no doubt that these are thoughts that you should not encourage, that will only worry you and fill you with negativity, right? They are perceptions that do not add up to anything and that, in that particular situation, would only be encouraging you to lose the opportunity to find a new job.

How could you counteract them?

Positive thoughts you could use to that end could be, in this case, the following: "I am sufficiently prepared for the position they are looking for at that company, so the chances of them hiring me are ample," "I know I can do well in the job interview," "I will do well in the interview and they will give me the job," "I am qualified for the position they are looking for, I have the knowledge and skills that are required."

One notices from the above example that the way to counteract negative thoughts is with positive ones, which by their very nature, completely contradict them from the beginning. "I will do poorly in the interview" is completely countered and transformed by the thought, "I will do very well; I can do it."

You should repeat the counteracting positive thought every time the negative one appears in your mind and even several times during the day, even when the negative thought does not appear for a while; just because it leaves you alone for a while does not mean that it has quieted down, do not allow it to regain strength. Ideally, you should counteract those negative ideas when you get up and before going to sleep, as well as the moments when those notions cross your mind.

Why This Simple Technique Could Help You?

It is valid to ask yourself this question.

The origin of any negative concept that appears to torture you is surely an idea rooted in your subconscious. It is an idea that you believe to be correct; you are convinced that this negative thought is real, or that the worst in X situation can happen, etc. Therefore, if you repeat a positive concept that counteracts it, you will calm your subconscious, and that will silence your repetitive thoughts. But that is not the best thing; the best thing is that by resorting to this technique constantly with the time, you will convince your subconscious, and you will transform your negative belief into a positive one, whatever it is. And this happens because the subconscious does not analyze the information it receives; the subconscious part of your mind does not discard as real or false a thought; it is neutral.

If you repeat that you are lousy at socializing, your subconscious mind will believe it, and consequently, you will be terrified, thinking the worst before an event in which you have to socialize. If you convince yourself, on the contrary, that you are capable of socializing, your subconscious will believe it, and you will avoid fear before a social activity; without the paralysis of fear, you will most likely start to improve your social skills.

So this is a mental conditioning technique. It can help you to change the perspective of your mind, conditioning it with the positive thoughts that you want; it can help you to change any limiting or negative beliefs that make you worry too much and that are usually the cause of your overthinking, it can help you to get rid of all negativity.

I recommend that you write down the negative thoughts that normally come to your mind and, based on them, create a list of positive concepts to counteract them. This way, you can use your list and repeat ideas that counteract the negativity in your mind and help you to condition it in a way that favors you. Although, in any case, if negative thoughts come to your mind that you don't have on your list, you can always take a moment to think of ways to counteract them.

What you should not get tired of is to counteract the negative thoughts that come to your mind by bombarding them with positive ones because, before you know it, the fact of repeating positive thoughts will convince your mind of the positive and push away the negative. Repetition is a cognitive restructuring technique, a topic that will be discussed later.

Identifying Your Negative Thoughts

To carry out satisfactorily the previous technique and many others that will be described during this book's development, you must identify your negative thoughts. It may be easy for you, but those thoughts torture you and rob you of peace, wander over and over again in your mind, and cause you anguish. But what if identifying your recurring negative thoughts is not so easy?

Don't worry.

In that case, you should take some time to analyze what is bothering you or what kind of negativity is going through your mind.

Identify the situation first, and think about why you have become anxious or some other negative emotion has invaded your mind.

Let's say you have a very important final exam coming up at your university, one that may decide whether you fail a subject or not. That situation probably distressed you or made you feel bad, don't you think so? It would be the most logical thing to do.

Once you have identified the situation, you should analyze the reasons why such a situation worries you, causes you distress, or causes some kind of discomfort.

In the case of the previous example, the reasons may be varied:

- You have procrastinated studying a lot and have very little time left to prepare.

- You think you are really bad at that particular subject.

- For whatever reason, you don't think you can pass.

The reason you discover will hide the negative thought you should deal with.

Why is that thought negative?

It may also be useful for you to check whether you have truly discovered the source of the negativity you are experiencing by asking yourself what emotion the particular thought you have discovered after analyzing the situation that triggered your discomfort has aroused in you.

Anguish? Frustration? Guilt?

Whatever emotion a particular thought arouses in you, it will harm you if it is negative. By analyzing this, you will realize how necessary it is to diminish or silence that thought in order to regain your peace of mind or well-being. This is important because, being aware of how much a thought is hurting you, you will have more motivation to push it away or fight it.

Whenever you feel anguish or any negative emotion, self-analyze, look for the cause and identify your negative thought because this will help you to be able to counteract it or face it effectively.

Do Things You Enjoy

Dedicating time to activities you like is another key to keeping away from your life and mind all negativity.

How much pleasure is experienced when you do something just for the fun of it, don't you think? How can that not help you, motivate you, and help you dispel the negative?

A clear example of how positive it is to do things we like is the passage of time. When we do something we like, we do not notice the passage of time; our mind is absorbed and totally motivated by what we do. The same cannot be said when we have to do something we do not like; from our perspective, time passes slower, and we cannot wait for it to end; we feel a lot of anguish if it is something we really dislike.

The chores and responsibilities of life make people put aside their hobbies and entertainment. Between the anguish and the general discomfort produced by excessive thinking, you have probably forgotten about yourself, about the things you like. Still, to remove the negativity from your life, you must take them up again.

Nothing like an afternoon doing something you love to do, to feel good and relax, and that's what you need, activities that produce well-being and that take your mind away from negativity. It could be anything: painting, dancing, going on a trip, baking, reading, writing, enrolling in that course you've been putting off, a sport.

What do you like to do that you haven't done in a while? It's time to set aside some time in your calendar for your entertainment and fun.

What activity do you enjoy more than anything else in the world? Practice it in your spare time.

Doing activities that you enjoy will be a balm for your anxieties and your negative emotions. It will be profitable for you and help you get your mind away from negativity. Do not deprive yourself of these activities; make time for them occasionally; your health requires it, and it is something you deserve.

You can not speak of someone truly happy who deprives himself of what he likes, but those who do what they like, are happy.

Spend Time With Your Loved Ones

In the same way as in the previous section, between the anguish, negativity, and busy life, time with family, friends, and loved ones is being left aside. And the truth is that spending a pleasant time with the people you appreciate has the same effect on the mind as a relaxing activity.

Give yourself time to share with the ones you love in your process of chasing away your negativity and allow yourself to do so. Make dinner and invite your relatives, invite them for a walk, anything, whatever you want. You will see how something so simple will bring light and calm into your life.

Practice Laughter Therapy

Very often, the negative emotions produced by the tendency to overthink make people forget to smile. When was the last time you did something just to provoke your laughter?

With your mind engulfed in negative thoughts, laughing is certainly not high on your list of priorities, but it can help you a lot.

Laughter is the opposite of negativity; laughter can release tension, relax you, and drive away harmful emotions (as well as thoughts that cause those kinds of emotions). So part of your path to freeing yourself from overthinking and removing negativity from your life should be to "Laugh" and engage in activities that make you laugh occasionally. It can be anything, an afternoon of comedy movies, an outing with extra cheerful friends, singing, reading jokes, or playing games (why not? It's good to indulge our inner child from time to time). Whatever it is, as long as the intention is just to laugh and have a good time.

It is contrary to all well-being to leave entertainment and laughter aside, don't do it.

Practice Gratitude

Becoming aware of the countless reasons you have to feel grateful is another way to ward off negativity.

Usually, the most negative, pessimistic and anxious people have forgotten about gratitude. They commonly focus so much on the negative that they become blind to the positive things they have in their lives, all those things for which they should feel gratitude. Therefore, practicing gratitude in your daily life will help you to remember the positive things you have been ignoring, which will help your mind not to focus only on the negative.

Gratitude is powerful. Becoming aware that there is so much to be grateful for can drive away negativity, make you realize that life is amazing in all its nuances, and that no matter what happens, there are many blessings in your existence. This will give you a more favorable and optimistic outlook on the world and life itself.

Take some of your time to make a list of all the things that awaken gratitude in you. Write down each and everyone: being alive, being healthy, having a family that loves you, the existence of what you are passionate about, having a home that serves as a refuge, and having a job or livelihood.

To get rid of the negative, it is essential that you become aware of what are those positive things in your life that make you a blessed person. If you think there is nothing, you must dig deeper and take some time off to analyze your personal blessings because there are blessings in your life, even if you believe there are not at this moment. I can say it with total certainty because one of those blessings is nothing more and nothing less than the fact that you are reading this right now, which means that you are alive, and the simple fact of being alive is already a miracle because it provides endless opportunities that are lost with death. How can you not be grateful for life?

If you are surrounded by people who love you and love you, that is something that makes you a fortunate person; if you are healthy, you are more blessed than many who are not; if you love to see the sunset and you can do it from time to time that is a blessing.

Analyze your big and small blessings, your accomplishments, the most special days you have experienced, and even the material things you are grateful to have. Anything goes as long as you feel gratitude.

By reading your personal gratitude list daily, you will not forget any blessings that bring light to your life. The important thing is that every day you remind yourself of the things that make you feel grateful so that you can get on track and achieve your goal of overcoming negativity. The things you feel gratitude for will motivate you to keep moving forward on your path to keep bad thoughts away.

At times when you feel more discouraged, do not forget to resort to that list; it will be a balm, you will see.

Every time something else happens to you that makes you feel grateful, enlarge your list. The more blessings you keep in mind, the better.

Positive Affirmations

Positive affirmations are very useful to take your mind off the negative. It is a technique that will help you diminish the effects of opposing thoughts or remove negativity from your mind.

Your mind will conceive as real that which you affirm with faith because the subconscious receives all the information that is given to it without contradicting it, as it has been exposed in previous lines (A topic that will be deepened in subsequent lines). In that sense, just as thinking that you are not enough can make you feel sad and incapable, or thinking that the worst may happen will make you feel anxious or worried, affirming positively will fill you with positive emotions. It will help you calm your mind when a repetitive thought or a string of unfavorable thoughts is haunting it or simply start your day or approach a situation more optimistically.

Turning the technique of positive affirmations into a habit can help a pessimist to become more optimistic, a person with a tendency to anguish to acquire a level of calm, to overcome bad habits.

Repeat the positive affirmations that suit you best at the beginning of the day and at any sign of negativity in your thoughts. If you want to silence a bad idea such as: "Surely today I will do terrible," your positive affirmations can be the following: "It will be a wonderful day; everything will go well for me." In case your mind tries to convince you that you are not enough, you can use positive affirmations such as the following to convince your mind otherwise: "I am enough," "I can handle all my responsibilities," "I am the size of the problem that comes my way," "I am intelligent," "I am a wonderful person".

You can make a list of positive affirmations that you want to imbue your mind with: "It will be an amazing day," "I will be able to deal with any problem that comes my way," "I am very diligent, and so everything will go well," "The people I will meet will be kind," "I always receive kindness from others".

These are not delusions; they are affirmations that will help you see the world from a positive perspective rather than with pessimism, which will never be flattering.

Positive affirmations are very similar to the technique explained above for counteracting your negative thoughts and conditioning your mind, but in this case, you will not be struggling to counteract a negative concept, although affirmations can help you to do so. They can fill you with positive emotions and vibes in general, so you should repeat them at the beginning of the day, in the evening, before going to sleep, whenever you want, and daily and not only when you need to because a thought is invading your mind.

Positive affirmations are powerful. Start this good habit and never give it up. It will be very favorable. It will change your life, you will see.

The Visualization Technique

As with affirmations, whatever you consciously visualize in your mind, your mind will conceive it as real and interpret it as real. The subconscious cannot differentiate as false the mental images product of the imagination; it conceives them as real. That is why you can convince your mind of what you want through this very powerful technique.

What does the visualization technique consist of? It is as simple as closing your eyes and giving free rein to your imagination, creating a scenario in your mind as positive as you want. That's why this is another technique that can help you ward off negativity. Of course, with your overthinking problem, you may find it hard to concentrate and perform this technique, especially if you have never used it before. Still, if you choose to relax before practicing it, you will certainly succeed.

There is no right or wrong way to practice this technique. However, I would recommend the following: You look for a quiet place, your room, or any place where you can relax without interruption. In that place, you can make yourself comfortable and close your eyes. If you can resort to relaxation techniques, it would be excellent. For example, place classical music, light an incense, control your breathing, inhale, hold your breath, exhale, and repeat until you feel relaxed. You can begin to imagine from that point, creating favorable mental images.

What Images Can You Create?

You can imagine anything, as long as it is positive. You should already know what to imagine before practicing the technique, for example, it may be your ideal day. You wake up in a good mood, arrive at work, start and end without problems... In case you are worried about something, for example, if you are worried about how you will do in a speech, you could visualize yourself giving the best of speeches, being praised and applauded by those present, smiling and speaking confidently...

What will this help you do?

To convince your mind that you will do well, that you can do something you would normally be afraid to do, to quiet fatalistic thoughts.

If your mind has been wandering to the worst-case scenario, visualize the best-case scenario. Fight negativity by imagining. Take power, convince your mind.

As with other mental conditioning techniques, if you resort to visualization daily, you can convince your mind of anything and fill yourself with positivity.

Whatever you imagine will fill you with emotions. Just as thinking that everything will go wrong will fill you with worry, imagining the opposite will make you feel more confident, more optimistic, more positive, better.

This technique can change your life if you make it a habit. More on this amazing technique later.

Make Time for Relaxing Techniques

If stress and emotions such as anxiety are contributing to your mind and life being filled with negativity, you should know that you have the option of turning to many relaxing activities and techniques that can take away that negativity and fill you with peace of mind and well-being.

When there is peace and tranquility in the mind, the body also feels good, and there is general well-being. Relaxing activities are very necessary, especially in modern life where stress often reigns.

Remove negativity from your life by making it a habit to do relaxing activities. Make this a priority if your life is especially hectic.

What Activities Might These Be?

- Meditation: In later lines, this topic will be deepened; however, you should know that meditation is the relaxation technique per excellence.

- Disciplines such as Yoga or Pilates (Their relaxing properties have been supported by science).

- Contact with nature (The serenity of nature is transmitted to the mind and body).

Or simply any activity that fills you with serenity and peace: Painting, swimming, dancing, music therapy. Any entertainment activity or hobby that you love will help you to relax your mind.

Give Yourself A Break From Negative People

The people you surround yourself with influence how you feel and sometimes your own behavior or attitude.

How could you keep negativity away by living all the time with pessimistic and anxious people who make it difficult for you to see the bright side of things and infect you with their anguish? You can't.

It is not about cutting all ties; it is not necessary, but on your path to healing, as long as you still cannot control your emotions nor have overcome the bad habit of overthinking, sharing too much with people with a tendency to pessimism and anxiety will interfere in your transformation process.

Let's suppose that after some effort, you manage to silence that inner voice that makes you overthink and, just then, you meet with someone extremely pessimistic who reminds you of those things you fear the most: "I heard that they will make staff cuts, maybe we will lose our jobs," "Inflation may increase in the next months," "I think it will rain and ruin our day." Your inner voice will likely come back to haunt you, and your previous efforts will be wasted.

Give yourself a break from this type of people while you overcome the bad habit of overthinking and, if it is within your possibilities, surround yourself instead with people who add to your life, cheerful and optimistic people who will recharge your batteries because just as some can infect you with pessimism, others can infect you with a more cheerful perspective of seeing the world and this is what is good for you.

They say that successful people only surround themselves with successful people; in that case, you should surround yourself preferably with optimists.

Give Yourself a Break From the "Morning News"

An unflattering practice for both negative and anxious people and people like you who want to overcome overthinking is to watch or read the morning news, especially those related to "happenings," which tend to be heartbreaking and, of course, negative.

It's fine to want to be informed, but if the news fills you with negativity or provokes excessive thoughts that fill you with anguish, you'll understand that it's not good for you. Stop impregnating your mind with those heartbreaking things that happen and that, in reality, you cannot change or, at least, give yourself a break from this type of news to recover positivity in your mind and life.

Combat Your Tendency to Perfectionism

If the origin of your habit of overthinking is the need for perfectionism and control, making mistakes on purpose or, failing that, doing things that you know you are not very good at will be helpful and will help you to keep negativity away.

Why not? Give it a try. It will help you realize that there is nothing wrong with not being perfect, to overcome rigidity and the need for control if these characterize you and are hurting you in your life by triggering your tendency to overthink.

Attend dance therapy, even if you consider that you were born with two left feet; paint a picture, even if you have never done it before and there is a wide probability that the result leaves something to be desired, send that email with a small hidden spelling mistake, omit even an accent in a word. Whatever, as long as it is something that takes you away from your comfort zone and your possibility of having all the control as you like it.

Planning things is an excellent option to get things right, but while you overcome your tendency to detrimental perfectionism, don't plan every last detail before you do something. At least allow yourself not to plan so meticulously activities that do not really require an excessively careful result.

It will also be useful to give each thing you have to do a level of priority and make a maximum effort only in the activities that require it; being able to delegate or leave for later activities that are not such a high priority.

Maybe reading this, you think you can't do it. Yes, you can let go if you set your mind to it; you can delegate, postpone, not plan so much and overcome your tendency to perfectionism if you set your mind to it. If it suits you, try it, and you will see that you can do it. The important thing is that you try and take action, even if you feel insecure, because, most likely, that's how you will feel.

Improve Your Self-Esteem

Your tendency to overthink may be due to a lack of self-esteem and a low tolerance for rejection that leads you to fear failure and always think the worst.

If your conception of yourself is poor, your inner voice will constantly be tormenting you with thoughts like "*I'm not enough*", "*I won't be able to do it*", and things like that. This will lead you to always think of the worst, to think of others when you have to face a situation that worries you, or that you don't think you are capable of.

"Surely I won't do it right; what will happen then?" "They'll probably reject me because I'm not nice; what will I do?" "What if I'm left alone?" These are examples of recurring negative thoughts that often invade the mind of people with low self-esteem. Moreover, a characteristic sign of low self-esteem is to feel that everyone is always evaluating you as a person. How to get rid of pressure like that? How to have peace of mind and drive away negativity? Hardly.

Is your self-esteem low? It is if:

- You constantly underestimate yourself. Faced with the challenges that are presented to you, you hardly feel capable.

- High self-demand: You always want to do everything excellent, and you constantly blame yourself for not being able to do things as perfect as you wanted.

- You feel insufficient and incompetent.

- You care too much about what people think of you.

- You are overwhelmed by fears related to your need to be approved: Fear of social rejection and failure.

If part of your overthinking problem derives from poor self-esteem, you should work on improving your self-concept on your way to overcoming overthinking.

Learn to love yourself. Your poor self-conception is only due to beliefs that you have allowed to enter your mind; what you think negatively about yourself is not reality. Change that conception of yourself, be kinder and more realistic when you evaluate yourself, and you will realize the wonderful and capable person inside you. There is no human being that is not wonderful and capable, and YOU ARE NO EXCEPTION.

The subject of self-esteem is so broad that delving into it too much would require another writing, a book entirely dedicated to that subject. However, the basic methods to improve self-esteem will be highlighted below. Follow these tips and you will improve your self-concept and gain the confidence you need to shine in your life, which will also help you leave behind the excessive thinking that torments you.

Become Aware of Your Virtues and Accomplishments

Low self-esteem will cause you to be practically blind to your virtues and achievements because what your mind will stand out and take into account will be your flaws and failures. Therefore, one way to combat low self-esteem and increase your pride is to become aware that you also have virtues and that you have achieved many things, that is, that you are also capable of achieving whatever you set your mind to.

Discover your virtues and achievements, and stop blinding yourself to them.

How to discover what your virtues are?

You will have to walk the path of self-knowledge. Evaluate yourself, and take some time to think about your virtues. Look for a list of examples of virtues on the internet and choose 5 of the virtues that you recognize that you have:

Are you kind? Are you generous? Are you sincere? Are you hard-working? Are you responsible? Are you punctual? Are you loyal? Are you patient?

In the world, there is no human being that does not have virtues; you also have virtues, discover what they are.

To help you discover your virtues you can also ask your closest people. Having low self-esteem, you have probably forgotten about them, but not about your closest people.

When you have discovered your strengths, write them down.

On the other hand, also make a list of your lifetime achievements, and write them down: When you graduated, when you learned that skill when you finally managed to socialize despite the fear you felt. All your accomplishments, from the smallest to the biggest, highlight them in this list.

The idea is that you read it daily so that you don't forget your virtues or your achievements.

Don't let your mind convince you that you are not special and wonderful because you are.

Overcome the Habit of Comparing Yourself

If your self-esteem is low, you probably compare yourself to others all the time. You will have to let go of that both to achieve the purpose of keeping negativity out of your life and to improve your self-esteem.

Does it do you any good to compare yourself to others? You know it doesn't, right? Most likely, when you do, you underestimate yourself. You won't find your own virtues and your capability in someone else. That person you are comparing yourself to may perhaps be amazing at X thing, and you are not, you are amazing at others, and that is absolutely normal.

We all have our differences, individual skills, and individual virtues. No one is perfect, no one is 100% skilled, and no one is 100% wise. That person with whom you compare yourself and who seems perfect to you and makes you wonder why you are not perfect or judge you, has flaws, has failed, has shades of gray, whether you can see them or not. There is no human being without flaws, as there is no human being without virtues.

Learn to value yourself as you are and, if you are going to compare yourself with someone, only with your own self of yesterday, with your past version, only with the intention of moving forward and improving your own self.

Every time you notice yourself comparing yourself, stop doing it, force yourself to stop, and focus your mind on something else, on any other train of thought.

Ask your loved ones or people close to you to make you notice when you are comparing yourself. If it is a habit for you, you may not notice it sometimes, but with the help of your close ones, you can notice when you are about to compare yourself and avoid it.

The important thing is that you manage to stop comparing yourself; this only brings you suffering and negativity, it does nothing for your personal development or to improve your self-esteem, so why keep doing it? Commit yourself to stop doing it.

Only set realistic goals (Evaluate your goals for yourself).

Part of your low self-esteem may be due to your habit of setting unrealistic and unattainable goals.

If you set unrealistic and even humanly impossible goals, you will obviously not be able to achieve them, and failing to do so will increase your level of low self-esteem because you will judge yourself for not having been able to achieve what you had set out to do.

If you never really had the opportunity to fulfill that enormous self-demand, is it fair to be hard on yourself or judge your capacity based on that goal that you could not fulfill even if you made an effort and gave everything of yourself? It is not fair. That is why this is something you should leave aside. Avoiding it and trying to set realistic and possible goals will not only not damage your self-esteem in an attempt to improve it but will also keep away possible negative thoughts that want to invade your mind product of self-judgment for not meeting your goals or any feeling of guilt without reason to be. You will be benefiting twice as much.

Become aware of whether the goals you set out to accomplish are achievable and possible. Evaluate whenever you set out to achieve them. What usually happens is that there is a tendency to set goals without carefully evaluating them; do this from now on. Whenever you set a new goal, evaluate it, ask yourself if it is humanly possible, and analyze if you have the resources to achieve that goal in the time you have set to achieve it.

Let's suppose that one of your goals is to lose weight. It would not be humanly possible for you to lose 20 kilos in one week, just as it would not be humanly possible for you to climb a big mountain if you have not had previous preparation.

It would be possible to lose 20 kilos, but not in a short period of time, at least not without resorting to surgery and without getting sick. Climbing a big mountain would be possible, but not without preparation; it requires training, increased stamina, and experimenting with smaller mountains.

Take some time to evaluate your goals. You can dream big, you can set any goal to reach, and you will surely reach it, but progressively. If your dream or goal is too big, break it down into smaller goals instead of trying to achieve something big all at once and end up getting frustrated and judging yourself as incapable.

Accept Compliments

Someone with low self-esteem hardly accepts compliments simply because they don't believe they deserve them. If you have a habit of underestimating yourself or making compliments small, leave that attitude behind. YOU DESERVE EACH AND EVERY COMPLIMENT YOU RECEIVE. So, on your way to improving your self-esteem and keeping negativity out of your life, from now on whenever you get a compliment, bite your tongue at the temptation to say something like, "It was nothing," and say, "thank you" instead.

By being grateful for the compliments you receive, you will be accepting them and, by accepting them, you will see yourself as deserving of them. This will have a great influence on your self-esteem; you will notice the change as soon as you begin to accept the compliments that you were previously inferior to, and you will be giving yourself your value.

You will encounter resistance; sometimes, you will not realize that you are rejecting a compliment. That's why it would be wise to talk to those closest to you about your desire to start accepting compliments from now on. That way, your close ones can make you see when you are rejecting a compliment, and you haven't realized it; it will be a great support for you.

Positive affirmations

Saying and repeating nice things about yourself will have a powerful effect on your mind.

Your low self-esteem may not let you appreciate yourself. The very fact that you have low self-esteem means that your mind is convinced that you have little value, but that can be changed with the help of positive affirmations, a powerful technique that I have explained before.

Affirming continuously and using positive phrases about yourself will influence the beliefs of your subconscious, you will convince your mind, and you will open the way to improve your self-esteem once and for all; remember that your mind conceives as real what you repeat to yourself.

Examples of affirmations to which you can resort with the purpose of raising your self-esteem:

"I am wonderful," "I am enough," "I am capable," "I am worthy," "I deserve love," "I love myself," "I am loved," "I am worthy of being loved."

Give Yourself Time and Affection

People with low self-esteem rarely give themselves tokens of affection, so start giving yourself affection and giving yourself time improves self-esteem.

Pamper yourself from time to time: Dress up not for the occasion or for anyone else but yourself, as you like; go to that spa, buy yourself that thing you liked so much and have been denying yourself because you consider it unnecessary, treat yourself to that chocolate. Show yourself love with actions and by dedicating time to yourself. ALL THE LOVE YOU GIVE YOURSELF YOU DESERVE, AND IT WILL HELP YOU TO GET RID OF NEGATIVITY IN YOUR LIFE.

Inner Reality Map

You probably know what the term NLP is or have come across it while reading. It is a widespread term that refers to an area of human knowledge that studies people's behavior and its bases. It is full of answers on how to think, act and feel in a healthy and effective way, how to change harmful thought patterns, limiting habits, improve communication and achieve productive personal development through the development of cognitive skills, emotional intelligence, and more. It is neurolinguistic programming, applicable today in education, business, sales, personal development, and much more to improve communication skills, cognitive and other skills that facilitate the achievement of various objectives.

The fact is that many techniques of Neurolinguistic Programming will help you to stop thinking so much because precisely this discipline is efficient to reprogram the brain and overcome all kinds of anxiety, blockages, and limitations. NLP will be useful because it will help you to calm your mind from any worry or fear that tends to make you think too much about things or from any behavior or thought pattern that harms you.

It is from NLP that the Inner Reality Map was born, a term that can help you solve your problem of overthinking.

And what is the inner reality map?

In NLP, reality is known as territory, which means that your reality is your territory.

Why is that?

Have you ever wondered why some people see a glass of liquid as half full, and others see it as half empty? That has to do with their perception of reality. For the one who sees the glass half full, that is his reality; for the one who sees it half empty, that is also his reality. And both positions are true.

If you ask someone which is the best means of transportation to move along the street and they tell you a car, that will be their reality, that person's perception of reality is that cars are better means of transportation than others, such as, for example, a bus or a motorcycle, but, another person may think that a motorcycle is the best means of transportation, even better than a car, and, probably has good reasons to think so based on their own experience. Both opinions will be motivated by these people's perception of reality, their experiences, beliefs, and thoughts.

An absolute reality does not usually exist except with scientifically proven facts. Otherwise, reality, how people conceive reality in their day to day, is conditioned by many things: by the education that was instilled in them, by lived experiences, by beliefs, and even by the state of mind.

Faced with a dismissal you and another person can act completely different, and that will be based on your inner map of reality, beliefs, education acquired, experiences, etc.

If you conceive the dismissal as a total failure, as a misfortune. That's how it will be, that's how you will perceive it, and that's how it will be for you. You will suffer because you will be dealing with the situation according to your own conception of reality. Still, a dismissal can be an opportunity for change for another person. This person, instead of suffering, can deal with the situation in a more optimistic way because he can conceive what is happening to him; with a more optimistic perspective, his inner map of reality leads him to conceive that situation with different nuances than yours, negative.

Same situation, different reactions motivated by the reality of each person, which is never the same in all situations between one person and another.

What could be the reason for an entirely negative conception of a dismissal?

There could be several reasons why a person conceives a layoff as negative from his inner map of reality. Perhaps a past experience made him consider that experience as a failure. For example, he was fired, and it was a terrible and negative experience from which he had a hard time getting out; perhaps it was learned, his family instilled in him the idea that being fired is extremely shameful and terrible. On the other hand, someone who conceives it positively probably has a positive reference to a layoff: someone close to him was laid off, and many other opportunities for improvement opened up for this person, or, perhaps, his family instilled in him the belief that it is always possible to find another job if one is lost, so he does not conceive it as something terrible, maybe not as something positive, but he will be able to conceive it with optimism.

Someone could have a map of their internal reality similar to yours, but never the same because this map is built during the course of life, and no one will live exactly the same life as another person: same experiences, same way of learning, same inculcated beliefs, etc.

How could knowledge of these situations help you overcome the harmful habit of uncontrolled overthinking?

By understanding that you build your own reality, you can make an important change in your mentality and free yourself from the weight of as many limiting beliefs as you have in your mind and as many fears as you have created in your head. Because they are part of YOUR TERRITORY, YOUR REALITY. If you change or transform your perception of reality, everything in you can change: thoughts, beliefs, habits.

What you would have to do properly is to understand how you create your reality, how what scares you so much or worries you so much and makes you think and think in negative without stopping is not an absolute reality but your reality, a perspective rooted in you. To achieve this, you would have to question your reality.

Everything related to the inner map of reality, its understanding, and the subsequent reprogramming of your mind so that you can create another reality that favors you, leaving behind the one that limits you, is a process of evolution in which a professional expert will accompany you to help you reach your personal evolution, to help you overcome your limitations. However, I will explain below how you can question your reality to try to change it for your benefit, in an attempt to silence all those thoughts that torment you, because yes, if you want to find a solution, why not help you to find it?

Question Your Thoughts to Help You Transform Your Reality

The following is a technique widely used by psychologists called debating (It is a cognitive restructuring technique; in subsequent lines, we will explain what it is about).

In this case, to carry out this technique, you will have to debate with yourself, questioning your thoughts to understand your personal conception of reality and how it may be affecting you.

How to carry out this transforming debate?

Its practical application is in the face of thoughts that are not very rational. That is to say, it will be effective if you carry it out before the appearance of those recurrent repetitive thoughts that make you suffer so much and that keep you awake at night.

When you apply this method to one of your recurring thoughts, you will be questioning it, questioning your reality, and that can lead you to transform it into a change of perception from negative to positive that frees you from your anxious, worrying, limiting thoughts. Remember that it has been commented in previous lines that most of those recurring thoughts, which attack your mind and fill it with negativity, do not have a real basis or at least they are not usually based on real and imminent danger. The catastrophic future that your mind makes you believe may not be as catastrophic as you expect; it happens that you are convinced of the worst. Still, by questioning your reality, you will be able to diminish the fear and worry and start thinking rationally without being blinded by that fear and worry. It will be a breakthrough to seek a change, to silence your excessive thoughts.

How to Question Your Thoughts to Change Your Reality?

The following are questions you should ask yourself in the presence of recurring negative thoughts:

1. Is this thought totally true? To answer, you would have to ask yourself another series of useful questions, such as the following:

- On what basis do I believe that this thought is true?

- What evidence do I have about the veracity of this thought?

- Is what I believe scientifically proven?

- Will it always happen this way, as I think, or is it just a matter of probability?

- Could there be an explanation other than the one I believe?

The idea is to think rationally and discover if the thought that invades your mind has a coherent and realistic reason for being or if it is only encouraged by fears and is absurd. You will surely discover in the process that most of your limiting beliefs and fears are only gigantic and true in your imagination. Most of the ideas that make you overthink don't have a reason to exist.

For example, if you feared that you might starve to death after a layoff before finding another job or source of income, you would have to question how rational it is to think that way. Why wouldn't you find another job or source of income after your layoff? Many people have found a layoff favorable because it has catapulted them to a better job or, to develop an entrepreneurial venture. Why wouldn't you have another income opportunity or the possibility of generating income from home, starting a digital or any other type of business?

If your biggest concern was not having any savings, surely you could resort to some loan, so how rational is it for you to think that you would starve? What proof do you have that you would not find another job? You would have to look for a job and go to interviews. It wouldn't necessarily be that easy, but would you really starve to death before you found another source of income? Don't you have anyone to help you with even a plate of food while you find a job? Your mother, a friend, a former co-worker, and even welfare sites could help you with that. Surely you could at least find something to eat daily to survive; you could sell some possessions to buy food. So, it is definitely irrational to think that your end would come by losing your job.

Another example:

Let's suppose that in your mind the thought, "They will stop loving me if X thing happens," you would have to ask yourself how rational is this way of thinking. On what basis do you think that way? Do you have proof? Does any scientific reasoning make you believe that or prove what you think? If you think you have proof, really, would all, absolutely all the people who love you, stop loving you if X scenario happened? It's highly unlikely.

IDENTIFY YOUR RECURRENT AND DAMAGING NEGATIVE THINKING AND QUESTION IT AS MUCH AS POSSIBLE.

2. How terrible will the consequences be if the terrible of my thought materializes?

This is another question you should ask yourself in your mental debate process to question the reality of your thoughts and reduce anxieties and fears.

- Would it be so terrible if the thing that worries you so much were to happen?

- How many areas of your life would it affect?

- Would it still matter 5 years from now what happens?

- Has anyone you know gone through something like this and failed to cope, or did they cope? How terrible was it for them?

Most likely, with the help of the answers to these questions, you will realize that what you think may happen may not actually turn out to have such terrible consequences. If you get fired, you won't surely starve to death; if you fail a subject, it won't be the end of your career; if you forget your speech, the consequences of it are unlikely to affect you for the next 5 years.

Think reasonably about your answers.

3.- What are the consequences of thinking like this for me?

Another question you should ask yourself in your internal debate and to help you change your perception of the unfavorable reality is this one, a question that will lead you to become aware of the damage that any of your recurring thoughts are doing to you.

To help you answer, you can turn to another set of questions, such as:

- Will this thing I am thinking help me in any way, contribute to me solving my problems?

- Does it do me any good to think this way?

- Does it bring me any positive emotion to think this way?

- What does it bring me?

At least most of the time you will discover that your recurring thoughts only hurt you and do nothing to solve your problems, so why encourage them? Being aware that your recurring thoughts not only hurt you but also that they do not provide the slightest solution will contribute to motivate you more to overcome them.

All this simple process will question not your recurrent thoughts by themselves but what has made you think that way, limiting and inculcated beliefs, fears, and your learned perception of reality.

To discover that what haunts your mind has no reason or basis for being, that you have no proof that what you think really will be or is that way, that the consequences of something you fear happening need not be as gigantic as you consider them to be and that, if what you fear happens, it probably won't matter in 5 years. Also, remember that thinking the way you think, more irrational than rational, hurts you and will help you a lot to calm your mind and reduce fears and harmful beliefs.

Your mind does not normally stop turning negative thoughts around and around because you do nothing to question their veracity, the exact magnitude of the consequences you believe you will have to face; everything will be more terrible in your imagination if you give control of your mind to your negative emotions. When faced with something that frightens you, if you give free rein to your imagination, you will think of a terrifying future of terrible consequences, and, as it turns out, the consequences of what we do or what happens to us are not usually as terrible as the mind thinks. But by questioning those thoughts, questioning your reality, you will be able to change it because you will be able to minimize your fears and worries. When you achieve this, you will see how those thoughts, a product of the conception you had of reality, stop tormenting you.

To take into account: This is a method that will require your maximum concentration, so when you are going to discuss a thought or a thread of thoughts that torment you, it is best not to be in a hurry or allow anything to interrupt you. Set aside time for this, it will not be effective if you practice this internal debate in a hurry. You could write down the negative thoughts that have been invading your mind during the day and question them before going to sleep or when you have some time to do it calmly, without the worry of having to do something later.

Cognitive Restructuring: How it Happens and What Obstacles Arise

To understand what cognitive restructuring is all about, you should first become familiar with the term cognitive distortions. Cognitive distortions are nothing more than the name given to irrational and automatic thoughts that are causing you to overthink and, in turn, produce profound discomfort.

Cognitive restructuring is a psychotherapeutic technique whose objective is to identify irrational thoughts and discuss them until they are changed.

What gives irrational thoughts so much power is that we rarely question or contradict them. On the contrary, we accept them, and by doing so, we are considering them real, even though they are not, we are giving them power over how we feel, over us. But it is not so simple to just contradict a thought when we believe it to be real, it is not so simple to identify a cognitive dysfunction, and to rethink personal reality.

The most basic forms of irrational thoughts are in:

- The tendency to guess what others are thinking: "He's probably going to dislike me a lot," "He's definitely going to think I'm clumsy," "He's surely going to act in X way," "He's definitely stopped loving me."

- Underestimating one's capacity: "I can't," "I don't know," "I'm not enough".

- Catastrophizing: Always thinking the worst.

Cognitive restructuring is, therefore, a way of transforming harmful and limiting thoughts into favorable thoughts, a way of correcting irrational thoughts or cognitive distortions so that they cease to be a problem or limitation in favor of maximum well-being through the modification of mental patterns. It is a technique that makes it easier to refute irrational thoughts until we realize how absurd they are. It involves a whole process with professional accompaniment because it can be really complicated to identify an irrational belief and to be able to refute it autonomously. However, professionals are sufficiently prepared and know effective techniques to change thoughts, achieve an effective transformation, and guide their patients toward a productive cognitive restructuring. However, this technique will be discussed in more depth below, and you can use it to overcome overthinking independently as well.

First of all, you should keep in mind that your irrational thoughts or cognitive distortions are a subjective way of thinking (remember the whole issue of the inner map of reality). This has already been discussed in the section on the inner map of reality. You perceive the world mostly subjectively, according to your perception of reality instilled by your upbringing, experiences, and beliefs. In fact, the inner map of reality is a concept that can help you understand very well what cognitive restructuring entails.

The basis of cognitive restructuring and the key for it to work is that you accept that your reality does not have to be the total reality, that you accept that your thoughts are only hypotheses, that you accept that your reality is based on your inner map of reality, on the subjective way in which you see the world and the circumstances as a result of your experiences, beliefs, inculcated knowledge, etc.

Have you already done it? Then you are one step closer to your transformation.

Cognitive restructuring as a process starts from these hypotheses (your conceptions of reality, your thoughts) and discusses and refutes them until it is possible for you or for the person who is in search of a change to realize that his or her thinking was not really rational, that it was not true or, at all, true as he or she thought.

 Suppose your irrational thought or cognitive distortion has to do with a deep-seated social fear. Faced with the possibility of having to face a social situation then, irrational thoughts would come to your mind, encouraged by your fear or anxiety. These would be of this type: "I am so lousy at socializing that I will make a fool of myself, nobody will like me, everybody will reject me." With the help of a cognitive restructuring process, those kinds of thoughts that would only increase your social phobia could be transformed into: "I can probably strike up some conversation with someone, but if that doesn't happen, it won't be so terrible." Or, suppose the irrational thought or cognitive distortion that often plagues you has to do with an absurd fear that your partner will leave you: "If my partner leaves me, it will be terrible; I will be so unhappy, and I might be alone." With the help of cognitive restructuring, this subjective hypothesis of the reality that is harmful to you could be transformed into a more rational and favorable way of thinking: "If my partner were to leave me, it might not be so terrible; it will hurt me, but I will be able to enjoy some time alone and be free until I meet, most likely, a suitable partner."

There are many cognitive restructuring techniques, and one of them has been discussed above as an internal discussion.

What is sought with cognitive restructuring is to change an initial thought, questioning it, something that can be done with this technique of internal debate.

Any procedure that leads you to refute an irrational thought, to objectively analyze its veracity, to change or transform it is a technique of cognitive restructuring.

We talked about internal debate before because it is a way of questioning reality, but we did not go into the whole process of restructuring your way of thinking.

How Can You Practice Cognitive Restructuring?

Various obstacles will make it difficult for you to change your assumptions, but keeping them in mind will help. You will have to combat those obstacles that will only hinder your cognitive restructuring process and hinder you from achieving your goal of overcoming overthinking.

Obstacle 1: "I think well, I am objective, and there is no more reality than what I see."

You will not be able to change your way of thinking if you are rigid to accept that there may be a reality other than what you believe.

You need flexibility; you need to understand that thoughts are hypotheses. Whether you think you are incapable of doing such a thing or you think you are capable, both thoughts or ways of thinking are just hypotheses; whether you think you will do well or you think it will be terrible, your thoughts are just assumptions, at least most of the time, when it is not something proven by science or with some basis.

We tend to believe that we are always objective in our thinking, but what if you are not being objective at any given moment? You won't know if you don't question your thoughts and assumptions. You won't be if you don't learn to be a little more flexible.

How do you do that?

Start at least by considering the opinions of others, even if they are different from yours, by giving a chance to someone else's opportunity... Also, by doubting your perspective to see things, take some time to analyze your way of thinking, verify what you base your thinking on, and the evidence you have for that.

Obstacle 2: "I can't help thinking that way, and it makes me feel so bad."

As long as you feel guilty, you will only distress yourself and fill yourself with negativity. Guilt can't help you get better, so try to let it go. It is not your fault that irrational thoughts come to your mind, but it is up to you to decide how to deal with them. Just focus on it.

Just by setting out to change the way you think, by following a process to transform your thoughts, you will be taking giant steps towards self-improvement, overcoming negativity and overthinking. It is what you have to do, and, therefore, there is nothing to feel guilty about; you are on the way to your improvement, you are doing what you have to do. You can't avoid your thoughts, and that doesn't matter because no one can avoid them, you can only control them, and you are in the process of learning how. Congratulate yourself instead of giving free rein to thoughts of guilt that have no reason to exist.

Dealing with guilt is another common obstacle to a cognitive restructuring process, but for the sake of the process, don't let that guilt limit you.

What can you do if you cannot silence the guilt?

- Meditate

- Practice Mindfulness

- Contradict that belief that makes you feel guilty and mentally repeat: "My thoughts are automatic, they come to me, even if I don't want them to, but I am not my thoughts, and therefore the guilt I am feeling has no reason to be and does not belong to me."

Obstacle 3: "I understand that I can think differently, but I don't think I can."

In your path to transform your thoughts, in your path of cognitive restructuring, when you are rethinking your vision of reality, when you are rethinking your negative thoughts in an attempt to convince yourself that they are not real or rational thoughts, you will most likely encounter this obstacle. You will find it difficult to think that you can change your way of thinking. Hesitant thoughts will come to your mind, such as: "I understand that I could think differently and that everything can improve if I change my perspective of seeing things, my own perception of reality; if I conceive everything negative, everything will be negative; if I conceive things more positively, it will probably improve; my outer world will change if I change my inner world, my irrational thoughts, my limiting beliefs... it is logical. But, I don't think it is possible for me because of how I feel, I can't believe in that way to solve my problem; maybe they don't understand me enough, if they understood me, they would think like me, that there is no solution. This is only fooling myself to change my thoughts".

You may think that by thinking this way, everything is lost, that by reasoning this way, you will not be able to change your thoughts, you will not be able to follow the healing process of cognitive restructuring and find your well-being, keep away the negative, silence your worrying thoughts. But you are wrong about that. Reflecting in this way is nothing more than an obstacle, and a very common one, on the road to change and cognitive restructuring. In fact, your thinking that way is even a good sign because if you are thinking that way, it is because you have been analyzing and learning about the process that could help you. You've become so interested in your well-being that you've read this book this far. Otherwise, if you didn't know that changing your inner world, your inner map of reality, and your thoughts is how you could change everything, then you wouldn't be asking yourself all these questions.

What you must do is follow the process of healing and transformation explained in these lines, and incorporate it into your daily routines, which moves you away from negativity, and allows you to question your thoughts so that you can control them, which leads you through a process of cognitive restructuring... These are some of the recommendations of this writing, even if you believe in the process from the beginning or not.

Most people who start a process of this type have countless doubts and are not entirely sure they can get the relief and improvement they need, but they give themselves the opportunity and start. They begin to change their habits, to meditate, to question their thoughts, and the process begins that way; the fruits they are getting help them believe in the process.

Do just that, do not give up without having started, start your process, change your habits, and carry out the cognitive restructuring techniques explained in this writing without thinking about it and thinking if it will work or not. On the way, you will gain faith when you notice improvements, you will see, but you have to be perseverant.

Ways to Carry Out Cognitive Restructuring

Use any technique that allows you to question your dominant negative thoughts and your perception of reality. Ask yourself and answer: what would happen if X thing I fear were to happen? How terrible could the consequences be? Inquire as to whether you have evidence for thinking X way, whether what you think is supported by science.

Most of the techniques developed in this paper will take you through a process of cognitive restructuring. Anything that makes you rethink the way you think.

Neuroplasticity

Neuroplasticity is the explanation of why repetitive negative thoughts become a habit, as well as one of the ways you can use to combat overthinking and remove negativity from your life.

With the help of neuroplasticity, you can give a brain restructuring that contributes to your positive transformation, that helps you think positively, leaving behind anguish, pessimism, clinging to control, and any way of thinking rooted in you that you have caused an excess of negative thoughts that become a problem in your life. Why? Because through the process of neuroplasticity, the brain can relearn anything.

How?

You have to understand what neuroplasticity implies, and this is nothing more than the brain's ability to adapt to any change from its interaction with the environment. In that sense, there is no doubt that our brain is resilient.

We learn from our experiences, don't we? How do we do it? The brain's functioning is complex, but a simple way to explain it is through neural networks.

It is common knowledge that there are many neurotransmitters or neurons in our brain. Neural networks are our neurons communicating.

When you learn something new, the neurons that process that information communicate it to the others, and thus, the whole brain is informed as well. When there is a repeating pattern, or new learning is reinforced, the set of neural networks that transmit the information related to that pattern becomes stronger and more deep-rooted.

Why does this explain the reason for repetitive thoughts?

When negativity is given chamber in the mind, when nothing is done to overcome it and negative and distressing thoughts are encouraged, then the brain adapts to that. There is no room for something new or positive, and the brain, which is neutral, ends up believing that all those negative and distressing thoughts are real, and that is where anguish and anxiety arise.

Giving space to negativity in the mind implies reinforcing the neural network that communicates those thoughts with each other, reinforces them, and makes them more solid.

There is no flattering neuroplasticity in rigidity, when you do not allow yourself to live any kind of novel experience.

What is convenient is to strengthen the neural networks so that positive thoughts are communicated, and to stimulate the brain's capacity to adapt to changes.

At this point, after having read all the lines up to here, you will not doubt that what you need to keep negativity and excessive thoughts from your life is precisely change. Stimulating neuroplasticity will help you because it will make your brain more and more prone to changes, or less resistant to them because, when neuroplasticity is not stimulated, the brain becomes very resistant to changes and, it is something difficult to deal with, a harder fight to improve.

It's worth taking some time to stimulate neuroplasticity, the change.

What precisely causes fear and anxiety? Limitations. When fear or anxiety is present and unchecked, we refrain from so many things: You probably refuse to meet new people out of fear or anxiety of possible rejection. You probably refuse every invitation to a social event for fear of having to socialize, you stop doing many things out of fear and anxiety. That doesn't encourage neuroplasticity and instead makes changes in your life more difficult. What you need is to take control so that you can leave behind the negative, ingrained beliefs and habits that induce you to overthink for the positive through neuroplasticity, which is transformation, and change.

If you stay in a comfort zone, stuck to the same old actions and routine, there will be no change for you in your mindset either; you will be trapped externally and internally in negativity. You must allow yourself other experiences for neuroplasticity to occur so that you can harness the full adaptive capacity of your brain to your advantage.

Your brain will become more resistant to change and less rigid if you experiment, if you allow yourself to do different things, live experiences that you normally reject, if you act beyond fear, if you step out of your comfort zone.

If you experience the new first hand, you will see that the world is not as terrible as your mind can conceive, but if you don't allow yourself the experiences, you can hardly convince yourself. The world will be terrifying in your mind because you don't allow yourself to prove otherwise.

How can you know that meeting new people isn't so terrible if you don't let yourself? Or understand that making a mistake in your speech is not the end of your career or the world if you refuse to give it out of fear? Or that you could find a better job than the one you refuse to leave, even if you don't like it, for fear of running out of livelihood?

Exercise neuroplasticity, allow your brain to experience changes from the interaction with the environment, create new experiences, pursue novelty, and expose yourself to your fears gradually. Live the different, do not hide...

Allowing the new to enter your life, starting, at least with small things, you will already be stimulating neuroplasticity in favor of the positive change you need.

You are probably very afraid of the new, but if you give it a chance, it will be a great change for the transformation of your mind and your maximum well-being.

Don't forget, keep in mind as a way of motivation that, being reluctant to the new will make your mind also reluctant to change your negative way of thinking for the way of thinking that really suits you, for a more positive or optimistic perspective of the world, the one that will keep away excessive thinking once and for all from your life.

With the above knowledge, here are some tips to activate the neuroplasticity process in your brain and help make it easier for you to adapt to new things and changes.

Neuroplasticity itself is a natural process; what you should try to do is to accept the change in your life. You can do it in the beginning with everyday and small things such as:

- Take a different route to work if you have adapted to always following the same route.

- Learn something new: To benefit from neuroplasticity, nothing like learning a new skill or acquiring new knowledge.

- Human beings never stop having things to learn: Enroll in that course you have been putting off doing out of fear, learn a new language, a new type of dance, how to play a musical instrument, about botany, astrology, ancient history, astronomy, whatever you want.

- Dare to talk to strangers and meet new people: Renew your social circle. If you find it hard to make friends or new acquaintances ask someone close to you to organize an outing with people you don't know and attend. It is sure to give you the opportunity to socialize, and undoubtedly that will help you stimulate neuroplasticity.

- Say yes to that invitation you usually turn down out of fear, or because it's about doing something you're not used to.

- Try a new dish, perhaps a typical dish from a country other than your home country.

The more new things you do, the more your brain will acquire the capacity to adapt to change, which is favorable to open the way to leave anxiety, pessimism, and overthinking behind.

Other activities that science has also endorsed as favorable for stimulating neuroplasticity are:

- Meditation

- Exercise

- Repetition

- Consistently performing mental agility exercises

Where we put our attention, neurons are activated:

Your neurons will be activated in the face of the negative if you constantly focus your attention on the negative. You will be reinforcing your negative thoughts if you do not neglect your attention on them, hindering the process of neuroplasticity. Therefore:

- Don't forget to repeat positive affirmations in the face of a negative thought to focus your attention on the positive and not on that negativity ingrained in your mind.

- Don't encourage your negative thoughts by allowing them to distress you. When these thoughts appear, make an effort to focus your attention on the present moment (practice Mindfulness, this discipline will be explained in the following sections), or meditation. Faced with a negative thought, you could meditate, focusing your attention only on your breathing to push that thought away.

Overcoming Anxiety

Not controlling anxiety will make you usually feel worried, will make you always think about the negative and the worst, will make it difficult for you to control fear, and will make you a victim of recurring negative thoughts that will only increase your anxiety and make it difficult for you to get out of the maze of negativity that it triggers in your mind. You will then understand that in your process of transformation towards a life free of negativity and excessive thinking, you will need to overcome anxiety. To do this, it is helpful to understand how it works. It is difficult to deal with what you do not understand, but, once there is understanding, the path to overcoming it becomes at least a little easier.

First of all, you should know that every person has felt anxiety at some time in life because anxiety is, like fear, part of the defense mechanism of the human mind. It is activated physiologically, like fear, when faced with a situation that seems threatening to us, whether there is a real danger or not.

Fear is triggered by imminent danger, by the possibility of getting hurt or dying in a given situation. It can also be triggered by imminent danger, although it is usually triggered by our fears, the future fear of something happening that we do not want to deal with. Thus, anxiety can be triggered, for example, before an exam that we want to pass because of the fear of not being able to pass or, before participating in a tournament, because of the nerves of being observed, the desire to win, and the fear of failure. It does not have to be a situation that can do us real harm; it is the fear of something happening that we are afraid of.

What triggers anxiety activates the defensive mechanism of the whole body, the anatomical mechanism that allows us to react faster to danger to defend ourselves or flee and thus survive. Anxiety often has a paralyzing effect. Experiencing it usually paralyzes us, and makes us not want to face situations or be able to do what we want, that is, it limits us. Also, when the anxiety is too much, it can be terrible and cause panic attacks, a collapse that is experienced and aggravates it much more.

Anxiety can be helpful because it alerts you to a possible future consequence, and on that basis, you may be better prepared to deal with it. For example, when facing an exam, anxiety due to the fear of not passing it may lead you to study more so that the consequence of not passing that exam does not occur.

You could never make anxiety disappear from your life completely because it is part of your body's functioning. Even the most confident person feels anxiety in any situation. The key, therefore, is to control it because not doing so is to live submerged in it, which is what you have to fight with.

Humanly it is not possible to live in anxiety, to live always in anguish, in worry and even less, suffering from panic attacks and dealing with so many worrying thoughts that it can create.

Living in anxiety is living in tension, being unable to relax, and not being able to find peace. You can say goodbye to this; you can overcome anxiety if it is a problem that afflicts you, and, in fact, you will have to do so in your process of freeing yourself from excessive thinking. Freeing yourself from anxiety in your process of freeing yourself from excessive thinking would be like catapulting yourself to your goal because if you overcome it, if you learn to control it, it will undoubtedly reduce your need to think about things, something you do because you feel worried. If that worry diminishes, you will not have to think about it. To overcome anxiety is, in a way, to overcome the habit of thinking too much about yourself.

The problems of anxiety have become so widespread that there are many methods endorsed by psychology that can help you to control it. I will describe them below:

Ways to Overcome Anxiety

Accept Anxiety

Recognize that you have an anxiety problem and that you need to deal with it; recognize that it is part of your life so that you can push it away.

It's not unusual for people to try to make themselves blind to their problem, to try to ignore it, but that doesn't work with anxiety.

Do you have anxiety problems?

Signs of anxiety include the following:

- Recurrent worry about the future or, constant restlessness.

- Feeling nervous or agitated

- Difficulty staying in the present because of recurrent obsessive thoughts about future situations that you are afraid to face.

- Difficulty sleeping

- Tiredness

- Irritability

- Panic attacks

Panic attacks occur when the body cannot cope with so much anxiety. And, from them arise signs such as the following:

- Intense fear

- Chest pain or pressure in the chest (Due to the presence of this sign, many people think they are about to have a heart attack while experiencing a panic attack, which increases the anxiety and its symptoms).

- Rapid heart rate

- Rapid breathing or difficulty breathing

- Tremors

- Excessive sweating

- Fainting (It does not occur in all cases, but it can happen in case of not being able to calm anxiety).

The explanation of the panic attack is that the brain erroneously activates the body's defensive mechanisms against an unreal danger, which can trigger your problem of excessive thinking; you probably have already experienced this terrifying experience. Once these mechanisms are activated, adrenaline is triggered in the body so that we can run away faster or defend ourselves better with the extra energy it gives to the body. Your brain will be trying to help you defend yourself from unreal danger with that extra proportion of adrenaline. It is this that speeds up the heart rate, which agitates the body so much as to accelerate breathing. All this will be motivated by anxiety and fear.

Do you identify with the above symptoms?

If you do, anxiety is an inconvenience to overcome in your life. There is such a thing as anxiety disorder, and suffering from it implies suffering such intense levels of agitation that it is necessary to turn to a professional. But, living with anxiety does not necessarily mean that it is this disorder, so you can try the following techniques to cope with your anxiety and, if it is not possible to overcome it, it would be best to turn to a professional because there is psychotherapy and medication that only a professional could prescribe and that could help you a lot.

If you think you need professional help, do not hesitate to seek it, your health must always come first.

Anyway, the following are the most efficient ways to overcome anxiety:

Unlink Any Negative Thoughts From You

Feeling guilty for any negative thought that invades your mind will only increase your anxiety. It will not bring any benefit; it is something you should try to avoid, and one of the ways to do it, if you make it a habit, is to unlink the negative thoughts that come to your mind, from yourself. This will also be a way of discrediting the automatic negative thoughts and detracting credibility from them. When you de-credit them, they no longer have power over you, over how you feel, you will have taken control if you succeed.

And how can you disengage from your negative thoughts?

Simply by taking the time so that, once an automatic negative thought appears that is making you anxious, say out loud or in your mind: "*This thought is not me, it is an automatic thought, but it has nothing to do with me, I am not this thought*". Repeat it several times, and do it with conviction. You will be removing the guilt from you while lessening the strength of the distressing thought in question.

To be able to carry out this exercise, you must propose to identify each negative thought that comes to your mind because only then you will be able to unlink it from you, you can.

Live in the Present: Mindfulness

Those who live in anxiety hardly live in their present since anxiety keeps them focused on the future, on imaginary scenarios, on thinking about the consequences, wondering what would happen if? Being a person to whom overthinking is a problem and who lives in anxiety, you will identify with it.

Do you find it hard to concentrate on what you are doing because your mind is suddenly filled with negative and worrying thoughts? Maybe it has happened to you that you are in your classroom listening to the teacher talking about an interesting subject, but suddenly your inner voice reminds you that there has been theft on your sidewalk, and you start to wonder if you locked the entrance to your house, or what would happen if you arrive and discover that your home has been broken into and your things have been taken.

In that case, you would physically be in class, your present, but, in your mind, you would find yourself traveling to the future.

If you live in anxiety, you will surely do many actions automatically while your mind is somewhere else, focused on everything but your present moment. This is why keeping your attention in the present is a big step in controlling anxiety.

Keeping yourself in your present moment will prevent anxiety from invading you, or, it will help you to reduce it if it is already doing its thing in your mind and you are worrying excessively for no reason.

You should know Mindfulness, a discipline whose objective is to maintain the focus on the present that is so effective that many adopt it as a lifestyle because it is very beneficial to live in the present not only to calm anxiety but to enjoy the moments. Life is precious for those little instants that we often miss because of being focused on the past or the future within our inner world.

Mindfulness is full of techniques that help keep the mind focused on the present. Of course, the first thing is that you want it that way and commit to keeping your mind more in the present and not all the time focused on the past or the future.

Mindfulness Techniques

On purpose, concentrate fully on the activity you are doing, several times during the day.

When you are overcome by anxiety, a negative repetitive thought, or simply when you want to, focusing continuously on the present will help you to turn that action into a habit, focus on what you are doing as if nothing else matters at that moment. Pay attention to whatever you are feeling at that moment.

Suppose you are taking a shower. To fully focus on that present moment and how it makes you feel, you could close your eyes and concentrate on the sensation of the water running over your skin, the warmth or the cold. Then you can start to sponge a soapy sponge over your skin and concentrate on that sensation as well, on the feel of the sponge and soap, on the scent, on what you can hear: the water hitting the floor, a distant conversation.

The idea is to immerse yourself fully in whatever you are doing.

Another example: if you eat breakfast alone, you can also use this technique, focusing on that moment. Every time you take a bite to your mouth, you can focus on the taste, slowly savoring it. What sensation does that bite awaken on your palate? Is it cold, hot, soft or pleasant? You can also focus on the smell of your food, its colors, and what you hear around you. Close your eyes while you chew.

This is a technique that works with any activity; you can focus your attention on whatever you are doing, washing the dishes, taking a walk, or drawing. Whatever it is, as long as you concentrate on that activity and nothing else, on what you feel while you do what you do, on everything you can perceive with your senses: seeing, smelling, feeling, touching, listening.

Of course, a thought may come to your mind to interrupt, and you may not be able to avoid it, and, at the moment of practicing this exercise, it is not convenient to fight against it. Fighting against a thought that invades you while practicing this exercise will take you away from your present completely and will ruin the essence of the exercise itself, it will distract you.

So, what happens if you are invaded by a thought while practicing this technique? What to do?

Don't judge yourself, don't worry, and don't feel guilty. Just deliberately refocus your attention on what you were doing before the thought in question appeared, close your eyes, and focus on the sensations.

In a moment of anguish when you cannot silence your mind of harmful thoughts, this exercise will help you find peace. Practicing it daily on the occasions you wish, you can train your mind to focus more on the activities you do, avoiding acting on autopilot. This will progressively help you to concentrate more and more on the present and less on your thoughts, helping you to overcome anxiety.

The First 3 Things You Can See, 2 Things You Can Hear, 1 Thing You Can Feel, 1 Thing You Can Taste

In moments of special anguish, when a repeated negative thought awakens in your body the annoying symptoms of anxiety without reason, or even during a panic attack, you can resort to this simple exercise that will help you return to your present moment and find peace. Thanks to it, you can control your anxiety, even if its. presence becomes strong in you.

What is this exercise about?

Like all Mindfulness exercises, its objective is to help you focus on the present and calm down.

When you know you are about to feel a panic attack or when you cannot silence the distressing thought, look around you, look for the first 3 things you can see that call your attention, and analyze them one by one. Let's suppose that one of those things is a painting on the wall, focus on it, on its colors, on its shapes; let's suppose it is a little bird, focus on the color of its feathers, on the way it flies. Then, do the same with two other objects that you can look at. Next, close your eyes and focus on two things you can hear, it can be anything, birdsong, distant conversations, or traffic noise. What can you hear? Become aware of at least two sounds around you. Still, with your eyes closed, breathe in and try to find a smell, even the scent of your perfume; what does it smell like at that moment? In the end, ideally, you should be able to find something to taste. In the absence of a piece of gum or candy in your pocket, taste the sleeve of your shirt, it is not important what you taste per se, only that you can focus on your senses at that moment.

When you finish, you will realize that the anxiety has either disappeared or has diminished, you will have managed to control it by focusing on your present and preventing it from continuing to move your mind toward a catastrophic future that has not yet materialized. That is the objective of this exercise, to bring you back to your present when anxiety is moving you to another place and you think you cannot avoid it.

Control Your Breathing

Deep breathing is a technique that can help you control anxiety by bringing peace to your mind while also relaxing your body.

As explained above, signs of anxiety include a rapid heart rate, rapid breathing, and tremors as the body's response to a worrying thought that it sees as an imminent threat. These signs further aggravate anxiety and, if left unchecked, can trigger a panic attack. Those who have experienced it know why it is important to avoid reaching this extreme because they are quite exhausting, those who have not lived that experience will do well to avoid it.

Precisely, deep breathing helps reduce the rigidity of the physical signs of anxiety to normalize the heart rate, reduce tremors and calm the breathing rhythm. When these physical signs of anxiety calm down, fear and anxiety diminish from the mind, and you calm down.

In the face of anxiety, you will need to relax, and deep breathing is an effective technique to do so.

Use the technique of deep breathing either when an excessive or repetitive thought worries you a lot and is making your anxiety arise, or daily, either before getting up, going to sleep or at any time of your choice, just in order to bring peace to your body and mind.

How to perform deep breathing?

It is a very simple technique, and for this, you will have to control your breathing. Before a strong anxiety attack, you may find it a little difficult to control your breathing. However, do not let that frustrate you; just keep trying.

Steps to effectively perform deep breathing.

- Let all the air out of your lungs

- Inhale deeply through your nose, let the air enter your lungs, and it oxygenates your mind and body.

- Hold your breath and mentally count to 5.

- Exhale, let the air out of your lungs through your mouth slowly.

- Mentally count 5 seconds.

- Repeat.

Do as many repetitions as you need to calm your nervousness. Deep breathing can take us to a state of relaxation so intense as to silence worrying thoughts, and it will do it gradually; you just focus on breathing. Close your eyes and do not worry; just focus on that moment, on nothing but breathing.

Remember, against your anxiety, breathe deeply.

Try to carry out this technique in a quiet environment or place, although you can practice it whenever you need it, or when the place where you are is not an impediment.

Sometimes you may not have time to use deep breathing if your anxiety is increasing rapidly, for example, during a speech. In that case, at least hold your breath for 5 seconds and then let it out slowly through your mouth. This will allow you to calm your nerves for the time being.

Progressive Relaxation Technique

This is another technique to suppress anxiety that works on the physical symptoms of anxiety. With its help, all the tensions and signs of anxiety such as tremors, rapid heartbeat, and breathing, are relaxed and calmed and thus also relaxes the body and mind. It is a technique whose effects have been supported by science, a technique that acts on the autonomic nervous system of the body, which is anatomically composed of two parts: the sympathetic and parasympathetic systems. To understand in a simple way what each one is in charge of, let's say that the sympathetic system is the one that is activated when we are scared or anxious before a real or imaginary danger, the one that tenses our body to defend us from a risk or flee, the one that puts us in a state of alarm (and is activated whenever you feel anxiety), while the parasympathetic system activates our state of rest or rest, relaxes the body to recover the energy lost by the activating stimuli when we are on the defensive, among other functions.

Anxiety tensions are weakened with this technique that activates the parasympathetic system. It is convenient to apply this technique when you feel that worry invades you; both body and mind will relax with its help.

Induce a state of relaxation by progressively undoing muscle tension in your body by following these steps:

- Acquire a comfortable position: Place yourself either sitting or lying down, but make sure that the position is comfortable. If you choose a chair, ideally, it should have armrests because you will need a surface to rest your arms on while performing the exercises of this technique.

- Breathe deeply: Close your eyes, breathe in through your nose, and hold it for a few seconds before expelling it through your mouth, wait a few seconds, and repeat.

- Relax as much as you can controlling your breathing before starting the actual exercise.

- Tense and untense the muscles to relax them: The next step of progressive relaxation will consist of tensing and untensing a series of muscles until the whole body relaxes.

- Stretch your right arm and clench your fists. Breathe in as you stretch your arm and hold your breath. Hold the pressure for a few seconds and the air in your lungs, then slowly lower your arm and unclench your fists while letting the air out.

- Repeat the same procedure with the left arm.

- Try to become aware of the sensations as you tense and relax your fists. As you straighten your arm and tighten your fists, you should feel the tension in your forearm, biceps, wrist and fingers. As you unclench your fists and lower your arm, you should feel the muscles become looser and more relaxed.

- Hold your breath and tense your chest. You should feel some pressure in the chest area. After a few seconds, relax your chest and let the air out of your lungs gradually. Be aware of how this action relaxes your body.

- Pull your shoulders back to keep some tension in that area, then relax them. Then lean your body forward, lift your arms with your elbows back and up to your back, and arch your back forward. This position will make you feel pressure from your shoulders to your lower back, be aware of this tension. Hold the posture and pressure, and then gradually relax until you return to the starting posture. Afterwards, be aware of how your muscles feel as you release the tension.

- Lower your chin to bring it toward your chest and hold the posture and pressure for a few seconds. Then relax the area, thus relaxing your entire neck.

- Arch your right foot toward your knee. This tenses your entire right leg and will put pressure on your foot, knee, thigh and buttocks. Feel the pressure, hold the pose, and then slowly relax by returning the foot to its original position. Repeat with your left leg.

- Without lifting your legs, squeeze your toes. Hold the pressure and then relax.

- Open your mouth as wide as possible. Hold for a few seconds (you can count to 10 mentally), then relax.

- With your mouth open, extend your tongue back as far as it will go until it rests in the bottom of your mouth. Hold the posture and then relax.

- Close your eyes by straining. You should feel the tension in the whole area around the eyes, the crow's feet area, and the eyelids. Then relax the muscles and return to the starting position.

When you finish, your whole body and mind should be relaxed.

You don't have to follow this technique exactly, the ideal is to practice it on all the muscles, but if you forget one, it's okay, but to memorize how to do it, and try to practice it in the same order each time.

Prioritize Your Time and Avoid Procrastination

Having little time to fulfill responsibilities or, the accumulation of responsibilities resulting from procrastination usually triggers anxiety, as well as excessive thoughts. If you have a lot of responsibilities to fulfill, you will find it hard to calm your mind, and it will probably constantly come up with anxious thoughts such as "What will happen if I don't finish on time?," "I will be seen as irresponsible and I will be fired," or similar thoughts. In that sense, it will benefit you a lot to manage your time, and leave behind procrastination and the habit of leaving to the last minute the completion of your tasks, if that is your habit.

How often have you told yourself you don't have time to do something? How often have you heard someone say they don't have enough time in the day?

If time is not managed, then 24 hours a day will not be enough. When there is a responsible management of time, the day is productive; it is enough to work, fulfill all kinds of responsibilities, and even for a bit of leisure and recreation, as well as self-improvement and personal development activities.

There are no more hours in the day for those who fulfill their responsibilities, go to the gym, and then have time for themselves, no. We all have the same 24 hours a day, the same 7 days a week. If your days are not profitable, it will be because you do not manage them well, take it for granted; and what is worse, probably, you waste time on unimportant things.

Activities such as checking social networks can mean the loss of valuable minutes and even hours that could help you accomplish activities that you should do, and that you are worried about not completing. When there is no time hierarchy, it can be wasted in activities such as the one mentioned above.

Manage your day-to-day, and you will see that you can do all your activities with enough time and calmly. You will say goodbye to worrying about the accumulation of responsibilities and the anxiety that it usually causes.

How to prioritize your time?

The first thing to do is to set out to do it. Buy a notebook or agenda for this purpose.

The best time of day to manage your time is in the evening. Take some time before going to bed to make a list of all the activities you have to do the next day. Then analyze all the activities on the list and think about which ones you need to do with the highest priority. If there are activities that you can postpone, do it to give top priority to those that need it; if there are activities that you can delegate, delegate them.

Many people find it hard to delegate, but, many activities can be delegated, and you should do it; you should learn to let go. Do it with at least one activity at the beginning; this way, taking that first step will be easier next time. Nobody can do everything; there are activities you can leave in the hands of others to have enough time to do other more important ones. Find out what they are.

Analyze your list well. Maybe you can leave half of that report to your classmate at the university or the writing of that email to one of your co-workers to give priority to the report your boss asked you for at noon.

Eliminate from your list for the next day the activities that you can postpone and delegate. The next thing you will have to do is to set up a schedule for each one. In this step, it is very important that you take into account that you are a human being who needs to rest and that you are sincere and compassionate with yourself.

One of the most common mistakes people make when trying to prioritize their time is having too many hours to perform an activity like a machine, and the result of this is not being able to meet the schedule created and a lot of frustration.

You are not a machine. Don't expect to be able to sit in front of your computer writing a report for 5 hours straight without a break. No matter how hard you set out to do it, you will hardly make it. In your planning, you must include breaks and also some leisure time because not considering some time for yourself will make you procrastinate.

It is also advisable to divide large tasks into small actions. So, for example, instead of setting out to write that report in 5 hours in front of the computer, you could spend an hour in the morning on that activity, then you could take a break, do another activity, and come back to it for another hour, in the middle of the morning, and so on until you finish it.

Any big activity should be broken down into small activities that will lead you to the end result.

Finally, when you finish planning your day, aim for the next day to accomplish your planning as well as you can. Of course, sometimes you will encounter unforeseen events, you can't see into the future, and there will be situations that will sometimes prevent you from sticking to your schedule to the letter, but, even so, the habit of planning your day will make them easier most of the time and will favor your process of overcoming anxiety.

Get Busy

Negative overthinking and anxiety do their thing in our minds, usually when we are unoccupied, like before going to sleep. If that is not the case and you notice that you begin to invade thoughts that fill you with tension and worry, get busy. Do something, anything, clean the house, tidy your room, paint, look for a recipe on the internet and try to prepare a new dish that you have not prepared before, go for a walk? In short, get busy.

Of course, the idea is not that you overload yourself with so many occupations that you can not even think, that will not magically disappear your anxiety or excessive thinking, but it will be useful for when your thoughts are about to trigger anxiety in you, because it will help you avoid them, to focus your attention on something else and not allow anxiety to invade you.

It is not a way to overcome anxiety, but it will help you to control it.

Sleep Hygiene

Not getting enough rest aggravates anxiety because lack of sleep triggers our body's protective alarm, which reacts as it would if we were in danger. In particular, lack of sleep triggers the release of cortisol, the stress hormone.

It is difficult to sleep when there is anxiety and excessive thoughts, but, you should do everything possible to have a restful rest because that will help reduce anxiety and keep away excessive thinking.

Try to have good sleep hygiene; here are some tips:

- Establish a fixed sleep schedule.

- Make your resting place appropriate to do so.

- Write down in a notebook your to-do list for the next day.

- Avoid exciting substances after mid-afternoon.

Do not Stay in Bed if You Wake Up in the Middle of the Night

If you wake up in the middle of the night, the best thing to do is to get up, walk around the room or house, get some water, sit up and wait for sleep to return. If you stay in bed, the probability that you will get nervous about not being able to sleep and that negative thoughts will invade you will be high. Thus, falling asleep will be more difficult and what is worse, you will be letting anxiety invade you.

Stay calm, do not stay in bed, and you will see that sleep returns.

Do not turn on your cell phone, TV or any electronic device when you get up, just walk or sit and wait.

Exercise

When we exercise or practice a sport, we get rid of tension from the body and relax the mind because, when we exercise or play sports, the brain secretes anti-stress substances such as serotonin, the hormone of happiness that keeps away anxiety. That is why exercising or practicing a sport is effective in the process of overcoming anxiety.

It does not have to be something intense; it can simply be moderate exercise: walking outdoors, cycling, swimming, or joining the gym.

If the exercise is practiced outdoors, its relaxing power is enhanced. Take it into account.

Relaxation

Relaxation is just the opposite of anxiety, that state of alertness and rigidity that activates mind and body so that we can defend ourselves or flee from danger; relaxation is calmness, tranquility. That is why in the process of overcoming anxiety, practicing exercises or doing relaxing activities is effective.

What activities can you do to relax your mind and body?

- Meditation

- Disciplines such as yoga or pilates

- Contact with nature

- Spa day

- Exercise

- Any activity you enjoy and calm you: painting, arts and crafts, walking outdoors, etc.

Confronting the Anxiety's Cause

When the anxiety derives from a specific cause, for example, when faced with having to speak in class in front of everyone, postponing the situation is pointless and only aggravates the anxiety.

A common attitude to something that causes anxiety is simply to avoid it. If you are anxious about crowded places, you will probably go out very little or avoid going to crowded places. If you are anxious about socializing, you will avoid going to that party you have been invited to. But, that does not help you to overcome anxiety, and, when it comes to activities that you cannot avoid like the one in the previous example, that of speaking in class because it could mean that you do not pass your course, then there is no possibility of escaping without negative consequences. That is, you could refuse to talk in front of your classmates, but, if that leads to lower grades or problems in your course, you will understand that it is not something you can simply avoid. You don't want to live on the run.

In that sense, one of the ways to overcome anxiety is to expose yourself to the reason that produces it, to do that which generates anxiety as best you can, and preferably gradually. This means that if you are very anxious about socializing, you should not go to a party of 300 people at once and see how everything goes because you will probably have a panic attack. The best and most effective would be to expose yourself gradually to the fear that triggers your anxiety: Dare to talk to a stranger, go to a meeting of few people and those you do not know too well, propose to socialize in a public place, but not so crowded, and so on.

Step by step, exposure by exposure, the fact of socializing would make you less afraid because each time you expose yourself to the cause of your anxiety, you will gradually discover by experience that what you feared was not as terrible as what was in your imagination. In the end, after gradually facing your fear, you could attend that social gathering of 300 people without anxiety, you will have overcome the anxiety, at least in terms of the specific reason that triggered it, and that you worked on by exposing yourself and facing your fear.

It is sought precisely with the exposure to the cause of anxiety to convince the mind that the situation is not as terrible as the imagination conceives it by living the experience.

In psycho-cognitive therapy, this is called exposure therapy, an effective therapy to overcome phobias, anxiety and even post-traumatic stress disorders. Of course, for very serious causes, the accompaniment of a psychologist or other professional is necessary for gradual exposure.

If you notice that it is too complicated to expose yourself to your fear, it would be best to go to a professional to determine the best way for you to expose yourself to that trigger of anxiety without it being counterproductive.

We cannot always do it alone, and that is why professionals are there to help us.

Mindfulness and Meditation Exercises

Schultz Autogenic Training

Exercising the mind voluntarily can influence the state of the rest of the body. This is the basis of this mind-body relaxation exercise, which has been scientifically proven to be able to reduce stress and anxiety levels and, therefore, to calm the physical signs of these ailments, which can also help to control excessive thinking, which is usually the result of high levels of anxiety.

It is also known as Schultz's self-hypnosis, and consists of a technique that is usually applied by psychologists in their patients, based on exercises that, through sensations such as weight, heat, heartbeat, calm breathing and coolness, encouraged by language and the power of imagination, induce a state of maximum relaxation.

The premise of this technique is based on the mind-body connection, on the fact that the mental state can influence the organism and, therefore, with imagination, mental peace can also be found.

This is a technique based on 6 exercises that must be learned progressively. It can be learned independently. Practice it several times a day, and you will certainly be able to do it sooner than you think, at least for the first 3 exercises, since the last 3 require a professional guide to obtain the desired results. In any case, the technique or the complete training will be explained below:

The Schultz Autogenic Training Step by Step

All the exercises will be explained below, but you must learn them in order. Only when you have mastered the previous one, practice the next one. Progressively advance.

The Environment

The main thing is to find a comfortable and quiet place to perform these exercises. Also, reduce the distractions in the place you choose to a minimum because you will have to concentrate to the maximum. If you do not manage to concentrate, the exercises will not give good results: Turn off the cell phone, close the door, ask not to be interrupted, and try to make the chosen room, a very quiet place, suitable for relaxation: Close the curtains or blinds, close the door, and turn off the light.

Also, choose a comfortable chair with armrests to practice this technique or, failing that, lie down on the bed comfortably. However, the latter is not so advisable because you may fall asleep and not be able to finish the technique.

The exercises

- Heaviness

The first sensation that is sought to awaken and relax the mind and body with the Schultz training is the weight. With the application of short, repetitive formulas and the help of your imagination, you should try to feel the weight in your extremities.

Start by breathing deeply. Inhale the air through your nose, hold it for 5 seconds and then exhale slowly so that the exhalation is twice as much as the inhalation. Repeat until you feel as relaxed as possible. Then, close your eyes and focus all your attention on your right arm. Try to imagine that your arm (or whatever limb you are working on) is made of lead, try to create just that mental image in your mind, that your arm is made of lead and is therefore heavy. Then repeat 6 times mentally, "I feel my right arm getting heavier and heavier". Try to concentrate on that feeling, to imagine it very heavy. If you concentrate hard enough, you will be able to feel how your arm starts to get heavier, that is what you will experience. Most of the initiates in Schultz's training quickly manage to feel the heaviness in their limbs, when you achieve it it will be time for you, without breaking your concentration, to repeat 6 times mentally or in a low voice: "I am very calm". The repetitions must be slow and calm.

Repeat the same process with your left arm, your right hand, your left hand, your right leg and your left leg. However, do not move from one limb to another if you have not really felt the sensation of heaviness, only move on to another limb if you manage to feel the previous one heavy.

To finish the exercise, breathe in slowly and open your eyes. It is important that the conclusion of the exercise is done calmly.

If you have already learned this exercise, it will be time to move on to the next one:

To take into account: While you are learning, you can only perform this exercise on one of your limbs, for example, the right arm only. As you progress, you should ideally proceed with several limbs.

- Heat

After the weight with Schultz training, you work on the sensation of warmth. In this case, you start in the same way as with the previous exercise, with deep breathing that induces relaxation and helps you to concentrate. Once relaxed, close your eyes and concentrate on your right arm again; imagine that warm limb. Remember the sensation of the sun's heat on your skin, and imagine that the summer heat is warming your right arm or the limb you are working on. Mentally repeat: "My arm (OR whatever limb you are working on) is feeling hotter and hotter".

It's no secret to anyone that heat does wonders for muscle tension and soreness. You should try to feel that pleasant sensation when you perform this exercise. Concentrate. Do the mental repetitions slowly. You should at any moment begin to feel the heat in your arm, and as it spreads to other parts of your body, it will be time for you to repeat: "I am very calm," slowly and at least 6 times.

Ideally, repeat the process with your left arm and both legs, but only change limbs if you really managed to feel the heat in the previous limb. Do not advance if you have not been able to feel it.

- Pulsations

Once you have mastered the previous exercise, the next one will be related to the pulsations of your heart. Start with an unhurried deep breath. Let the air oxygenate your body and calm your body and mind, then close your eyes and concentrate on your heartbeat. You can create in your mind a mental image of your heart beating calmly for greater effectiveness. Then repeat at least 6 times, slowly and calmly: "My heart beats calmly". If you do this exercise well, your heartbeat will indeed calm down because studies have shown this to be true.

When you feel very calm, then repeat mentally: "I am calm".

Finally, take a deep breath and open your eyes.

- Breathing

From this exercise, there are not usually good advances without the accompaniment of a professional. However, if it is your desire, you can try it. After all, your determination and concentration could help you to bring the exercise to a successful conclusion.

Once you have mastered the pulsation exercise, the next one will have to do with your breathing. Start as with all the previous exercises, controlling your breathing, consciously breathing in through the nose, expelling through the mouth slowly, and repeating until you feel very calm. At that moment, repeat with your mind about 6 times: "My breathing is becoming calmer and calmer". Keep your focus always on your breathing, and you will notice that it does indeed slow down. For greater effectiveness, you can imagine floating along with your slow breathing. When you feel calm and feel that your breathing is quite calm, repeat mentally: "I am very calm" at least 6 times before stretching your limbs and slowly opening your eyes.

- The abdomen

Having assimilated the previous exercise, you will continue to master relaxation now in the area of the stomach or abdomen.

Breathe deeply and relax, close your eyes, and try to imagine that your abdomen area is a source of heat capable of radiating warmth throughout your body. Then mentally repeat at least 6 times: "My abdomen radiates warmth". Once you feel the warmth in that area, mentally repeat: "I am very calm," before finishing the exercise.

- The mind

The last exercise is related to the mind. Control your breathing and close your eyes. Try to concentrate on your mind, try to locate it somewhere on your forehead. Then, with your focus on that spot, mentally repeat at least 6 times: "My mind is fresh". Try to imagine that a nice cool breeze is blowing through your mind and calming it down, you should feel a little coolness in that area of your body. When you feel a certain sensation of well-being and mental freshness, repeat mentally about 6 times: "I am very calm," before finishing the exercise.

Repeat this training several times a day and daily until you have mastered the exercise. Do not rush or get frustrated if you take too long to master one of the exercises to move on to the next, this is a process that can take a long time and should never be rushed. What you need is to be consistent and go at your own pace.

Visualization or Guided Imagination

As mentioned in previous lines, creating mental images consciously has a strong power of mental conviction due to the neutrality of the mind, to its functioning, to the fact that the mind sometimes does not separate the real from the imagination and conceives as real, whatever you imagine.

The guided visualization technique consists of consciously creating mental images that lead to sensory impressions. By guiding your imagination, you will be able to experience different sensations, experience emotions, etc. The imaginary will become physical because, as the mind conceives as real what you imagine, then with your mind, you can create situations that make you experience emotions of all kinds. Most commonly, guided visualization is used for relaxing purposes. In fact, the technique of guided visualization is used by mental health professionals to reinforce treatments for anxiety, overcome fears, and more.

With the help of guided visualization, you can reduce your fears, gain self-confidence, silence any worrying and negative thoughts, and acquire a new habit. This is a very versatile technique.

When the mind is convinced, you are capable of anything, and therein lies the power of this technique.

Understanding what it is and how it can be so effective will, perhaps, be easier with examples:

Suppose you've been thinking about the fact that you have a social gathering coming up that you'd like to attend, but you're really scared, you're not confident in your ability to socialize, you're afraid of being rejected, doing something awkward, or generally speaking, that it will go really badly. Definitely, thinking about it a lot will awaken fear and anxiety in you, but, if you use guided visualization to create mental images where you can visualize yourself socializing incredibly in that social gathering, laughing with strangers, being accepted and having a good time, then the fear and anxiety will diminish because your mind will believe that what you are imagining is real, and in that way, you will have convinced your mind that you can socialize and therefore you will feel more confident to attend the social event.

Thus, in this simple way, you can silence any negative thoughts that might be torturing you with an imaginary catastrophic event at your next social gathering.

On the other hand, suppose you are terribly nervous because your driver's license test is coming up, and you don't feel prepared. Using guided visualization to imagine yourself driving perfectly and passing your test will make you feel more confident the day you have to take the test, and that confidence will make you perform better and, therefore, most likely lead you to pass.

It will definitely be easier for you to pass it feeling capable than doubting yourself even to turn on your car's flashing lights.

On the subject of relaxation, if you feel really stressed and do not have time to go for a walk in nature or do some relaxing activity, you can use guided imagery to visualize yourself in a quiet, serene place that also brings you serenity.

It is as effective to relax in the imagination as it is to relax by doing any activity.

Only with guided imagery will you be able to reach an essential level of relaxation.

Guided Visualization Step by Step

I will explain to you below the step by step to carry out the guided visualization technique for relaxation purposes, to free yourself from stress and anxiety that any negative thought has awakened in you. But there is no formula for guided visualization; you can imagine anything, and you can use it for many different purposes, such as those mentioned above.

- The place you choose to practice guided visualization should be suitable for full concentration on the technique to be performed: It should be calm, as quiet as possible, and pleasant.

- It will not be possible for you to apply this technique effectively if you cannot create mental images, and, you will not be able to if you are distracted, if there is a lot of noise, if you are interrupted.

- Make yourself comfortable: Preferably seated as, lying down you may fall asleep.

- As with virtually any relaxation technique, start with deep breathing. Just focus your attention on your breathing, and try as much as possible to quiet your mind.

- You can imagine any scenario that suits you. If your goal is to relax with the help of guided visualization, you can imagine any place that relaxes you, or, you can imagine yourself doing something that relaxes you. However, since the most effective is usually a serene place in nature, then you can imagine a forest.

The following will be just one example of how you can carry out guided imagery:

Imagine that you are walking barefoot in a thick forest, around you perceive lush and beautiful trees, covered with flowers of all colors, the blue sky is beautiful and clear, a bright sun illuminates the place, you are barefoot, then you can feel the fresh grass under your feet. If you close your eyes you perceive the pleasant sound of singing birds lulling you, in the distance, you also hear water running, you walk following the sound, and you arrive at a crystal clear stream; you enter it, and you feel the fresh water on your skin. The water is so crystal clear that you can see fish swimming, you close your eyes, and the sound of the stream and birds singing are still perceived, now you can smell wet grass, and the smell pleases you.

Possibly many just by reading the above description, can imagine what is described and get an idea of how relaxing the situation can be, well, if you can voluntarily imagine all that, convince your mind that you are surrounded by nature, free of all negativity, you will undoubtedly be able to relax no matter how stressed you were before starting the exercise.

Self-taught you can resort to this technique whenever you want. You can also find on platforms such as Youtube, for example, all kinds of videos with specific relaxing guided visualizations, which include sounds of nature and calming music to accompany the process.

The important thing is that you achieve your purpose of imagining a totally relaxing scenario that helps you to relax your mind as well; therefore, you can also resort to these guided videos if you prefer.

What Is Rarely Explained About Guided Visualization

At this point, you know how powerful this technique is, how much it can help you achieve any purpose you set out to achieve, reduce fears, and say goodbye to overthinking and anxiety. And that it is a technique that is not only powerful but simple.

However, not everyone finds it easy to create mental images and that is what very few people explain when it comes to the guided visualization technique. It won't be effective if you can't create the mental images that help you convince your mind of what you want. Fortunately, you can train your imagination, did you know that?

In that case, if, when trying to carry out the guided visualization technique, you notice that it is not possible to imagine anything or to create mental images, you would have to first, train your imagination, go little by little, try first to create small images in your mind instead of trying to create a whole scenario, experience small sensations with the guided visualization instead of expecting to experience a more complex set of sensations.

You would have to go little by little, gradually...

Once mastered, once you can create mental images, then you can fully use the guided visualization technique to achieve your goals.

Step by Step to Train Your Mind to Create Images

Follow the same steps explained above to carry out the guided visualization technique to achieve an optimal state of relaxation through the practice of deep breathing.

- *Practicing with the sense of sight*

The first exercises to practice and develop mental visualizations should be related to the sense of sight since it will be the easiest one to recreate in your mind.

Try to imagine for at least 20 seconds, the following:

o An orange

o A ball

o A car

o A cotton candy

o A bird

Don't overexert yourself; simply try to recreate in your mind each of these objects. Think about them; think about how an orange looks like, its shape, its color, its texture...

Concentrate as much as possible you should be able to visualize each object.

It will be easier to visualize only one object rather than a whole scene or landscape, so this exercise will help you to stimulate your imagination.

- *Practicing With the Sense of Hearing*

Once you have mastered the previous technique, once you manage to create mental images of simple elements in your mind, practice being able to hear also what you imagine, since, with the guided visualization technique you should try to stimulate all the senses.

In this regard, imagine:

- Try to hear different people calling your name: Think of the sound of your mother's voice when she calls you, your father's, your brother's, a dear friend's. Remember the tone and timbre of the voice and concentrate fully on that memory; you will surely manage to hear as if they were calling you.

Then imagine:

o The sound of water falling from a waterfall.

o The sound of a cat meowing

o The sound of traffic

o The sound of a blizzard

With this same procedure, you should continue to stimulate the rest of your senses. For the sense of touch, you could imagine:

o Stroking a sheep's wool

o Touching a cotton shirt

o Walking on fresh grass.

It doesn't really matter what you try to imagine as long as they are simple elements because it would be starting from the most basic to be able to advance and create more complex mental images.

If it is difficult for you to create mental images that help you to effectively carry out the visualization technique, spend at least 3 minutes a day training your imagination; this time will be totally worth it, it can benefit you a lot.

- Meditation

One of the relaxation techniques par excellence, and perhaps the best known, is precisely meditation. Through it is possible to reach a state of deep relaxation, which reduces anxiety and stress levels, calms the mind of any recurring negative thoughts, and even improves sleep.

By meditating, it is possible to quiet the rational and conscious mind and connect with the inner world and the unconscious mind to calm it down.

Making meditation a habit brings about a lot of well-being and will contribute to your transformation process to leave harmful overthinking behind. Meditating brings inner and mental peace.

How to meditate?

Take into account, first of all, your clothing and the place where you will practice meditation:

o Clothing: To practice meditation, you should be as comfortable as possible or, you will find it difficult to concentrate. In this sense, wear loose clothing preferably, and take off your shoes.

o Place: The important thing is that in the place where you decide to meditate, you can concentrate and relax. A quiet room, your garden.

The place should be as quiet as possible, and the temperature should not be too cold or too hot.

As with any meditation or relaxation exercise you want to practice, you should minimize distractions: Turn off your cell phone and ask not to be interrupted. Try to make your meditation effective by taking care of preparations that can help you meditate effectively, elements that help you keep your attention focused only on your meditation process.

If you choose a room, you can resort to relaxing music or some recording of nature sounds or other soothing sounds. You could also light some incense as the pleasant smell will help you relax your mind.

The Meditation Step-by-Step

Choose a comfortable sitting posture to meditate. The lotus posture is the best known, the universal posture of meditation, but, it is not mandatory to adopt it. What is important is that you sit with your back straight.

Close your eyes and begin deep breathing.

Deep breathing is always useful before starting any relaxation exercise because it improves concentration.

Keep your mind focused on your breathing. Put your hand on your stomach as you breathe in and out so you can feel the air going in and out of you. Breathe in through your nose, count to 5 mentally, then let the air out through your mouth slowly, feel your stomach deflate. Embrace the sensation. Repeat throughout the process.

Some recommend leaving your mind blank, but the truth is that you may not be able to. It is while you keep your mind focused on your breathing that you will encounter resistance. Thoughts will come to you that you don't want to interrupt the moment, and what you need to do when that happens is to turn your attention back to your breath. Just don't let those thoughts take your focus away or judge yourself for not being able to let your mind go blank. Very few people can do this, and meditation doesn't need to be effective.

Choose a phrase as a mantra and repeat it mentally while

controlling your breathing. The most commonly used mantra is "Ohm" because, within the discipline of meditation, its sound is known as a way to fill yourself with pure and renewing energy, but you can choose any positive phrase as your mantra.

As your goal will be to overcome the excessive thoughts that dominate your mind, you could choose some like the following: "I am peace," "I am at peace," "Peace is with me," "Peace reigns in me," "I feel so peaceful". Repeat your mantra mentally with great faith while continuing with deep breathing. Let those beautiful words convince your unconscious mind that all is well, that there is only serenity around you.

Adding the sound of a Tibetan singing bowl to your meditation routine will be favorable, since the vibration of its sound is very relaxing.

Meditation itself is just this if we talk about a step by step; it may be simple, but its effect is very powerful. Start with just a few minutes and gradually increase your meditation time. To see results, you should meditate daily. Once you start, you will not want to stop this effective practice.

The Role of the Subconscious in the Mind

At this point, you already know that what you have to face to overcome overthinking is your mind and your inner map of reality, which makes you see your environment and what surrounds you subjectively and negatively. It fills you with fears that cause you anguish, limiting beliefs, and demands that only cause you harm. And, basically, all that is stored in your subconscious.

Very often, the example of an iceberg is used to talk about the subconscious mind. And there is no better way to represent it, being the tip of the iceberg, the visible, the conscious mind, and everything that is at the bottom of the sea, hidden, that is not perceived with the naked eye, is the subconscious.

We think we forget things, but the truth is that we do not; all information we acquire is stored in the brain, but not at the tip of the iceberg, but deep inside. You have a lot of information stored in your subconscious, information about practically the entire base of experiences that you have lived throughout your life.

The functioning of the brain is quite complex, and there is still much without scientific explanation, but it is true that what we do, the way we act, the decisions we make are largely influenced by our subconscious mind; we do not realize it, but it is what happens.

In the subconscious mind is where fears, phobias, negative limiting beliefs, and traumas end up stored.

If you give it control, if you let your subconscious mind take automatic control of your mind, then you will be condemning yourself to let your fears and negative thoughts grow and control your life. This is why you must take control. The usual thing is to let the subconscious mind take automatic control, but it is not in your best interest.

You can access your subconscious mind. Professionals achieve the connection through techniques such as hypnosis, but you could connect with your subconscious mind through meditation.

You can benefit from trying to change your most ingrained negative beliefs in your subconscious by combining meditation with the repetition of positive affirmations that contradict your most ingrained negative thoughts, which lead your subconscious to a positive relearning, to a restructuring.

Also, basically every technique and recommendation along this writing will help you with the objective of re-educating your mind, of transforming your unfavorable thoughts into favorable, positive, beneficial ones, that is to say, by thoughts that free you from excessive thinking.

Conclusion

Congratulations for having completed this work. Congratulations for having sought the help you needed because, if you were interested in the content of this book, there is no doubt that you wanted to solve your problem of excessive thinking. Your well-being was within your objectives, and you sought it. That was the step you had to take at first; it is a step that many do not dare to take because, despite the discomfort that excessive thinking, insomnia, and anxiety can cause, many find it difficult to realize that they have a problem to face and overcome, as they have become accustomed to excessive thinking and begin to conceive it as their normality. But, it is not fair that overthinking becomes normal; it is not fair that it limits you, that it triggers so many negative emotions, such as low self-esteem. It's not something anyone should have to deal with forever. And it definitely won't be your case if you don't allow yourself to just take the knowledge gained from this writing at face value.

It is now up to you to put into practice what you have learned here, and take action. That is what is required, that you start the path towards the transformation of your thoughts and peace of mind. As with any road to travel for the achievement of objectives, you will encounter obstacles, and, in this writing, you have been prepared for them, so you can overcome them; even if you are afraid, even if you think you are weak at this moment, you are definitely not.

There is a lot of strength inside you. You have the flame of willpower, a flame that is an inherent part of the human being and that we all can activate when we want something and when we have enough motivation. And, if you have read this far, you already know that there is much more, beyond so much uncertainty, stress and worry, beyond turning things over and over again. How can you not be motivated to put an end to such a negative habit as overthinking?

Your lifetime is running while you ruminate with your thoughts; you are missing your present by thinking so much about things, by torturing yourself with so many worrying thoughts, you are missing opportunities that your habit of overthinking does not allow you to take advantage of. Fear is not fulfilling its positive role in you; it is not protecting you or helping you, it is harming you, but, with determination, even if it scares you at first, even if you do not believe you are capable, even if some of the techniques to overcome excessive thinking and negativity do not seem so effective if you follow the process and the recommendations learned here, you will not improve, you will transform yourself. You will go from being insecure, fearful and anxious to being the best version of yourself, and you will acquire confidence, self-esteem and serenity; all these qualities will undoubtedly lead you to happiness. That is what is important, that you conquer your mind in favor of happiness because that is what it is all about, that you achieve happiness.

Overthinking has been keeping you away from happiness, but you can get back on track when you realize your strengths.

Again, congratulations. I know you will succeed, brave reader.

If you want to share your opinion and enter to win a Kindle on "how to increase productivity", scan this QR Code using your phone's camera or go directly to this link:

www.philipgibsonbooks.com

THANKS!

Printed in Great Britain
by Amazon